2004 POET

ONCE
A RHYME

IMAGINATION FOR
A NEW GENERATION

Middlesex
Edited by Lynsey Hawkins

 Young**Writers**

First published in Great Britain in 2004 by:
Young Writers
Remus House
Coltsfoot Drive
Peterborough
PE2 9JX
Telephone: 01733 890066
Website: www.youngwriters.co.uk

SB ISBN 1 84460 426 8

Foreword

Young Writers was established in 1991 and has been passionately devoted to the promotion of reading and writing in children and young adults ever since. The quest continues today. Young Writers remains as committed to engendering the fostering of burgeoning poetic and literary talent as ever.

This year's Young Writers competition has proven as vibrant and dynamic as ever and we are delighted to present a showcase of the best poetry from across the UK. Each poem has been carefully selected from a wealth of *Once Upon A Rhyme* entries before ultimately being published in this, our twelfth primary school poetry series.

Once again, we have been supremely impressed by the overall high quality of the entries we have received. The imagination, energy and creativity which has gone into each young writer's entry made choosing the best poems a challenging and often difficult but ultimately hugely rewarding task - the general high standard of the work submitted amply vindicating this opportunity to bring their poetry to a larger appreciative audience.

We sincerely hope you are pleased with our final selection and that you will enjoy *Once Upon A Rhyme Middlesex* for many years to come.

Contents

Joshua Burkmar (10)	17
Rebecca Horton (8)	17
Lauren Nichols (8)	18
Megan Kyri (10)	18
Daniel Moore (8)	19
Thomas McVey (8)	19
Samantha Leeman (7)	19
Daniel Smith (8)	20
Gemma Srnecz (7)	20
David Jacob (7)	20
Charlotte Salisbury (7)	21
Alex Gasson (7)	21
Owen Wheeler (8)	21
Ellie Usher (7)	22
Jack Ellingham (7)	22
Ellen Davis (8)	22
Tom Bulshaw (7)	23
Hanna Chaudhry-Green (8)	23
Callum Bond (7)	23
Charlotte Avis-Winter (7)	24
Daniel Chamberlain (7)	24
Luke Bagnell (7)	24
Lucy Gannon (8)	25
Lauren Reeves (8)	25
Jordan Jennings (7)	25
Charlotte Ross (11)	26
April Cousins (8)	26

Crane Park Primary School

Thamina Miah (10)	27
Bryoni Bowers (11)	28

Echelford Primary School

Abigail Pearce (10)	28
Samantha Collins (10)	29
Mikey Bishay (10)	29
Philip Legg (11)	30
Jasmine Parsons (11)	30
Abigail Pearce (10)	31
Sam Culverhouse (11)	31
Courtney Hatt (10)	32

Edgware Junior School

Kessia Destifanis (8)	57
Robert Stevens (9)	57
Jodie Cottol (10)	58
Nosaiba Drera (10)	58
Ceri Ellis (10)	59
Keeley Don (8)	59
Jordan Turner (9)	60
Farva Baqir (8)	60

Holy Trinity CE Primary School

Spencer Mogge & Callum Woodbridge (9)	61
Oliver Matthews (9)	61
Ben Jones (9)	62
Malak Fouda (10)	62
Andrew H Johnson (10)	63
Jenny Murray (10)	64
Jade Soiza (10)	64
Monica Ashby (10)	65
Samara Deng (11)	65
Harshini Ranchhod (10)	66
Karina Smith (10)	66
Luke Wilburn (11)	67
Hakim Sakaraka (11)	67
Elise Jones (10)	68
Zoe Byrne (11)	68
Jessica Leigh (11)	69
Nikhil Chavda (10)	69
Dominic Williams (7)	70
Will Ashby (10)	71
Milly Bowen (11)	71
Sarah Hunt (7)	72
Sally Boultbee (7)	73
Shefali Parmar (11)	74
Steffi Lai (10)	74
Tom Wheatland (7)	75

Pinkwell Primary School

Grant Gilbert (11)	75
Aron Ahluwalia (10)	76
Sarika Vashi (10)	76
Hafsah Khan (10)	77

Priya Kapur (11)	78
Sonal Bhatt (10)	79
Aroosa Sheikh (10)	80

Raglan Junior School

Loren Adkin (7)	80
Olivia Watts (8)	81
Bradley Phillips (7)	81
Oliver Lewis (7)	82
Emily Campion (7)	82
Roberto Moscattini (8)	83
Luke Christodoulou (8)	83
Samantha Whitbread (8)	84
Michael Rose (7)	84
Jessica Morrison Nicol (7)	85
Sahel Manuchehry Wahed (7)	85
Jack Smith (8)	86
Tom Hassan (7)	86
Sharlene Gandhi (8)	87
Deeya Dulhumsingh (8)	88
Dominic Celimon (8)	88
Shona Burke (7)	89
Andrea Michael (7)	89
Shania Sinanan (7)	90
Jordan Whynn (7)	90
Nina McGarvey (8)	91
George Gaylor (8)	91
Canberk Sar (7)	92
Amy Godfrey (8)	92
Lauren Moret (8)	93
Lucy Fleming (7)	93
Josephy Doyle (7)	94
George Platt (8)	94
Ramin Daswani (8)	95
Ellie Richards (8)	95
Eve Rosina Gidley (7)	95
Fateha Ahmed (7)	96
Ayana Charles-Mathurin (8)	96
Anna Boyes (7)	96
Marianna Savva (7)	97
Matthew Bouchacra (8)	97

Adnan Aufogul (8)	97
Alexander Georgiou (7)	98
Joshua Lever (8)	98
Songul Uzun (8)	98
Katie Palmer (8)	99
Maria Tryphona (8)	99
Rianna Wray (7)	99
Elliott Scott (7)	100
Holly Evans (8)	100
Thomas Cocks (7)	100
Libby Pearce (7)	101
Abbie Vivers (7)	101
Jamie Egan (8)	101
Trixibel Gurjao (8)	102
Shazeea Masud (8)	102
Remmy Ezeabasili (7)	102
Edward Razzell (8)	103
Lois Panayiotou (7)	103
Chantelle Sheehan (8)	103
Peter Whitehead (8)	104
Joshua Cann (7)	104
Thaynara Tocantins (8)	105
Maximillian McKone (8)	105
Kyriacos Nahlis (8)	105
Benedine Antwi (7)	106
Millie Rickleton (7)	106
Sean Kelly (7)	106
Tommy Little (7)	107
Harriet Brown (7)	107
Emily Coelho (7)	107
Michelle Eghan (8)	108
Heidi Welch (8)	108
Stephanie Stevens (8)	109
Ben Salvi (7)	109
Jake Smith (8)	110
Sophia Evangelides (8)	110
Chloé Green (8)	111

Reddiford School

Roshni Adatia (10)	111
Afzal Roked (9)	112

St Nicholas CE Primary School, Shepperton

Alex Harrison (9)	159
Elliott Hinds (9)	159
Declan Naylor (9)	159
Elliot Carter (9)	160
James Parsonage (9)	160
Dominic Hillman (9)	160

St Teresa's RC First & Middle School & Nursery, Harrow Weald

Pierce O'Connor (11)	161
Evlyne Oyedokun (11)	161
Jamie Brogan (11)	162
Sean Matthews (11)	162
Ailish Carolan (10)	163
Michael Kennedy (10)	163
Shanice Thomas (11)	164
Christy Casey (11)	164
Rachel Cunniffe (11)	165
Danny McIntyre (10)	165
Holly Cook (10)	166
Luke Burke (10)	167
Jordan O'Neill (11)	167
Keri McEvoy (11)	168
Joanna Lewis (11)	168
Fraser Simpson (11)	169
Treston McKenzie (11)	169
Tamara Joanes Dias (10)	170
Simon Teer (10)	170
Samantha Vanderputt (10)	171
Chantelle Frampton (10)	171
Abbie Carey (10)	172
Lauren Lehane (10)	172
Sarah Innes (11)	173
Tristan Thomas	173
Rebecca Hine (11)	174
Raymond Cullis (10)	174
Callum Murchan (11)	175
Jake Embley (10)	175
Michael Baggs (10)	176
Laila Sheridan (10)	176
Natasha Sendanayake (10)	177
Sean Derbyshire (10)	177

Daniel Clarke (10)	178
Bethany Pelling (11)	178
Anthony Lewis (11)	179
Ryan Cox (11)	179
Anita Anthony (11)	180
James Okeyemi (11)	180
Grace Barber (11)	181
Earan Grey (10)	181
Christian Fraser-Williams (11)	182
Nathanael Munir (10)	182
Christina Baker (11)	183
Jordan Carroll (10)	183

Twickenham Prep School

Jemima Davey (9)	184
Nikki Thind (8)	185
Victoria Barnes (10)	185
Louisa Bolton (10)	186
Alicia Gumpert (8)	186
Jasmine Swan (10)	187
Nidhi Puri (7)	187
Jessica Manning (11)	188
Edward Smith (9)	188
Charlotte Smith (10)	189
Lorn Jackson (10)	190
Jake Gorridge (9)	190

Vaughan First & Middle School

Tove Hubbard (9)	191
Anushka Ahmad-D'Mello (9)	191
Hary Ilanko (10)	192
Victoria Body (9)	192
Shamima Ali (10)	193
Brian Greene (7)	193
Samia Siddiqi (9)	194
Karishma Tailor (10)	195
Layla Alami (10)	196

Whiteheath Junior School

Sarah Key (8)	196
Caroline Cousins (9)	197
Nehal Doshi (9)	197
Georgia Russell (10)	198
Carl Pullem (10)	198
Jessica Leese (9)	199
Christopher Musgrave (10)	199
Robyn Wetteland (8)	200
Christopher Demosthenous (9)	200
Kirstie Guildford (7)	201
George Leen (9)	201
Dominic Apuzzo (7)	202
Verity Ball (10)	202
Danny Lewis (8)	203
Candice Devine (9)	203
Jared Smart (8)	203
Lauren Wilson (9)	204
Ciara Murphy (9)	204
Billy Stark (9)	205
James Skinner (10)	205
Emma Watson (9)	205
Rebecca Gyetvai (9)	206

Wood End Park Community School

Emma Pereira (11)	206
Ellis Rogers (9)	207
Iveta Olahova (11)	207
Kayleigh Bowdrey (11)	208
Daniel Miles	209
David Watford (10)	209
Reece Saunders (10)	209
Nadine Bowen (8)	210
Teleasha Bogle (8)	210
Luke Innes (9)	211
Macayla Benoit (9)	211
Amber Cooley (11)	212
Charlene Svinurayi	212
Suraj Davdra (9)	213
Lakiesha Griffith	213
Vijay Kocher (11)	214

The Poems

The Moon And The Sun

Going through the shiny river and I feet a little shiver
The moon looks like the trees and feels a little freeze.
The moon looks at the dog's kennel and sees a little sparkle,
Way up in the sky.

The moon sees a little fly and says, 'Why?'
I feel like I'm flying way up in the sky
I always say goodbye.

The moon is so bright in the night that it gives me a fright
I say goodnight and begin to sleep tight.

Emma Ross (10)

Snow Is . . .

Slippery soft as a baby's skin,
Glistening in the rough wind,
A blanket of snow, lovely and cold,
Beautiful countryside full of white snow.

Cold and icy all through winter,
Pretty and cuddly too,
Windy and beautiful all through winter,
Soft in a fluffy bed.

Shabnam Qurashi (7)
Alexandra Junior School

Snow

Snow is as soft as a cuddly teddy,
It is as white as the white swan and duck,
It comes from space,
To fall on your face,
Snow is as chilly as you're standing in the North Pole,
The ice is as hard as a high wall,
The ice is as pretty as a rose,
You have to wear your gloves, hat and scarf
To keep you extra warm,
Throw a snowball on the floor,
Then have a race across the door,
Make an ice cube big and tall,
Do not try to pick it up or you might fall.

Priya Anjali (8)
Alexandra Junior School

Snow Is . . .

Snow comes softly drifting down,
On the snowmen all around,
Now the air has filled with magic,
Snow comes falling down, not a whisper,
Not a sound,
As boys go skiing on the road,
Cold snow comes slowly from the blue sky,
Snow is as fluffy as a teddy.

Surpreet Minhas (8)
Alexandra Junior School

Snow

Snow is soft like a swan's wing,
Snow feels like wool, soft and furry,
Snowflakes like diamonds.

People fall on the ground and make angel shapes,
Traffic jams everywhere,
No one can get out of the jam,
People making snowmen.

In Iceland, they are making igloos and
Getting wood for the fire.
Water turns into cold and slippery ice,
Children throwing snowballs but not ice balls,
People ice skating in the cold icy place.

Everyone wearing a scarf, hat, gloves and a warm coat.

Manjulika Rall (8)
Alexandra Junior School

Snow Is . . .

Snow makes ice hard,
Slippery and cold,
Snow is soft as your bed,
It's fluffy as wool,
A snowball is crushing in the wind,
But slowly it melts away and
It will be back next year.

Farhana Irshad (8)
Alexandra Junior School

Snow Is . . .

Snow is as white as a blanket,
Flying away in the wind,
As silent as air drifting down,
Very slowly on the town.
The snow is fluffy and very beautiful,
People make footprints on a winter's day,
This is a fairy falling here and there,
Everywhere the ice is frozen all around
On a cold and frosty morning,
The ice is thick and soft with lots of covered layers,
The snowmen are melting,
The people are warm,
The fires are lit and the hot tea comes to us.
Snow, snow, snow,
Snow is falling down,
Snow, snow is falling down,
Soft now, snow, snow, snow.

Zareen Bhatti (7)
Alexandra Junior School

Snow Is . . .

Snow is white and drifting down,
As snowflakes are falling down,
Snow is fluffy like cotton,
People playing ice skating on a slippery day,
Snow comes softly, people make snowmen
Outside in their garden, it is freezing,
People are making igloos,
Where the Eskimos live,
Snow is white and drifting down.

Shreya Gohl (8)
Alexandra Junior School

Snow Is

Crispy ice crunching,
Igloos all around you,
People making snowmen and snow-women.

People shivering,
Windy weather and winter too,
Soft snow slowly drifting down.

Bavan Kaur Gahir (7)
Alexandra Junior School

Snow Is . . .

Chilly and cold, and crunchy and white,
Falling quietly in the night,
It covers the treetops and the roofs,
A soft and beautiful sight.

Chandni Rhanna (7)
Alexandra Junior School

Snow Is . . .

Snow is soft and ice-cold,
Snow is falling from the sky,
It makes us happy and smile,
Snow is bright and white,
But it gently melts away . . .

Zeyad Sadek (8)
Alexandra Junior School

Soft Slippery Snow

Shiny snow drifting down onto rooftops,
Snow is silently falling to the ground,
Once snow has fallen, silence can be found,
Snow is fluffy freezing my hands,
Looking like a pure white woollen blanket,
Dropping down from the fresh air,

Soft, snowy, slippery, soothing snow!

Abhinaya Chandrashekar (7)
Alexandra Junior School

Soft Slippery Snow

Shiny snow drifting down onto the rooftops,
Snow is fluffy and freezing and makes me cold,
Snow is silence like calmness,
Snow is falling down to the ground,
It covers the ground like a blanket.

Anita Atuma (7)
Alexandra Junior School

Snow

Snow is small and you play snowballs,
Snow is soft and it turns to sleet,
Snow is fun and freezing cold,
Slish, slish the snow's all gone!

Damian Freeman (8)
Alexandra Junior School

Snow Is Falling Down

Snow is soft,
Snow is cold,
Snow is silently drifting on the ground,
When my hands are hot the snow melts in my hand,
When I wake up snow's silently drifting down,
Snow,
Snow,
Snow please come back,
I want to have fun with you.

Anisha Arun Singh (7)
Alexandra Junior School

Snow Is . . .

Snow is white snow, is soft,
Snow is freezing when you cough,
Snow is like drizzling balls from space,
In a place where I can play with my sleigh!
Snow is frozen water,
When snow turns to ice
You will turn nice.

Rajashree Alwar Mandayam Krishnian & Abdur Rahman (7)
Alexandra Junior School

Snow Is Falling

Snow is slippery, slippery as ice,
It makes you slide all the way down the ice,
Snow is funny, funnier than anyone.
Snow looks beautiful like a white blanket,
It is a lovely thing to play with in the world.

Pavan Ubhi (7)
Alexandra Junior School

Snow

Snow is slippery, sliding through my fingers,
Snow has a white woollen feeling,
Snow is the sound of children making snowmen,
Snow is watery when it starts to melt,
Snow makes my wellies wet,
Snow makes me cheerful when I am unhappy,
Snow falls silently, drifting down.

I love snow!
You love snow!
Everybody loves snow!

Snow!

Khushali Parshotam (7)
Alexandra Junior School

Snow

Snow is slippery, sliding through my fingers,
Snow has a white woollen feeling,
Snow is the sound of children making snowmen,
Snow is watery when it starts to melt,
Snow makes my wellies wet,
Snow makes me cheerful when I am unhappy,
Snow falls silently drifting down.
I love snow,
You love snow,
Everybody loves snow.

Mandeep Virdi (8)
Alexandra Junior School

What Is Snow?

Snow is slippery slidy,
Snow is fluff from the sky,
Snow melts on my hands,
Snow looks like white rice,
Snow,
Snow,
Snow!
Snow,
Snow,
Snow!

Yara Chaer (8)
Alexandra Junior School

What Is Snow?

Snow is slippery,
Snow is soft,
Snow is slidy,
Snow gives you a cough,
It is watery,
It is puddles,
Snow looks like a ball made out of wool.

Isahak Hashi (8)
Alexandra Junior School

Snow, Snow

Snow is a fairy falling down,
Landing on your windows,
Crispy and crunchy where you walk on it.

And you can go mountain climbing,
You can go on your snow mobile out for a ride
And go ice skating down the mountain,
You can build a snowman.

Snow comes falling down.

Amir El-Aouadi (7)
Alexandra Junior School

Snow

Snow falls on red rooftops,
When you step in snow,
You slip as you go when you
Have a nice hot cup of tea.
Snow is white like a white
Cotton blanket.

Reuben Sanger (7)
Alexandra Junior School

What Is My Teacher Like?

Fast-runner
Report-giver
Friend-maker
Laughing-joker
Top-sporter
Smile-giver
Talking-partner
Good-skipper
Secret-keeper
High-scorer
Progress-maker
Happy-trender
Problem-solver
Paper-sticker
Homework-giver
Super-actor
Paint-lover
Book-reader
Game-player
Picture-drawer
Great-speller
Mind-thinker
Story-writer
God-prayer
God-praiser
Food-eater
Delicious-baker
Great-designer
Message-texter
Hair-dresser.

Ria Marwaha (10)
Andrew Ewing Primary School

I Am . . .

I wrestle and roll
I lap and lick
I turn into foam
And make people sick.

I wear away rock
I guzzle up sand
I swallow up ships
And creep over land.

I float up as clouds
I fall down as rain
I soak through the Earth
Then come back again.

I glide over pebbles
I gurgle in streams
Run down in rivers
And open your dreams.

I once was a mist
I once was the sky
I once was a tear
Which filled up your eye.

I stung you with salt
I made your wood rot
I've been making waves
Ever since the year dot.

I am water
The water in the sea
Listen to me!
Listen to me!

Priyanka Sethi (11)
Andrew Ewing Primary School

Mrs Kelley

Chocolate-eater
Fast-runner
Kind-person
Fast-marker
Book-reader
Clever-brain
Loud-speaker
Fast-thinker
Forgetful-brain
Intelligent-person
Friend-maker
Science-co-ordinator
Science-expert
Curly-hair
Silver-earrings
Kind-carer
Card-giver
Recorder-player.

Prabkiran Bal (10)
Andrew Ewing Primary School

Sweets

S ugary and sweet,
W afers are just one kind of these delicious stomach fillers,
E xcitedly taking you on a sweet journey,
E nthusiastically made,
T eeth rotting,
S oft and creamy.

Aqib Iqbal (10)
Andrew Ewing Primary School

Spring

Spring comes once a year,
There are lots of things to hear.
The sun shines with glee,
The birds are all free.

Relaxing rainbows and the hot breeze,
Green leaves appear on bare trees.
New lambs, new flowers,
And the new spring showers.

Now the days are lighter,
Sunnier, happier and brighter.
When the children run to the park,
The dogs give a loud bark.

Spring showers on the streets,
Lots of children get some treats.
Go to the beach on comes sun lotion,
While you look at the deep blue ocean.

Maryam Ahmad (11)
Andrew Ewing Primary School

Valentine's Day

Valentine's Day is the day of love,
When Cupid watches everyone from above,
Chocolates, gifts, cards and flowers,
That's how love shows its powers,
Red roses to lovers and yellow to friends,
This loveable process never ends,
Therefore,
Roses are red and violets are blue,
Hope your Valentine loves you too!

Sapna Tomar (11)
Andrew Ewing Primary School

Rain

Looking outside,
The rain is like a tide.
Pouring rain,
Wish I was in Spain.

The rain pours down,
While I sit and frown.
The clouds are grey,
I want to go out and play.

I feel so blue,
There's nothing to do.
The rain keeps coming,
I keep humming.

Raindrops fall,
Can't play with my ball.
Splashes I hear,
Nothing to fear.

Sitting by the fire,
Can't pump my bike tyre.
Can't go out for a ride,
Have to stay inside.

Although the rain pours,
And I have to stay indoors.
We can't live without rain,
Let me make that plain.

Jaspreet Kler (11)
Andrew Ewing Primary School

The Good Bad Day

I woke up this morning,
And fell out of bed,
Bumped into the wardrobe,
And hit my head,
Fell down the stairs,
And broke my leg,
And that was the end of that.

I woke up next morning,
And got out of bed,
Got clothes from the wardrobe,
And patched up my head,
Hopped down the stairs,
With a cast on my leg,
And that was the end of that.

I woke up the next morning,
The sun was bright,
I looked in the mirror,
It gave me a fright,
I couldn't see my body,
Or my head,
And then I noticed
I was dead!

Shaun Newport (11)
Ashford CE Primary School

Little Red Fox Limerick

There was once a little red fox,
Who lived in a big brown box,
When he was fox years eight,
He went to open the gate
And sorry to say he got chickenpox.

Bethany Ann Doggwiler (8)
Ashford CE Primary School

Turtle's Secrets

Water splashes against the rocks,
And makes a crash like thunder,
The tide goes up,
The beach is hidden,
Under the saltwater waves.
The moon is like a diamond,
In the coal-black sky.
The sand is like golden crumbs.
A giant turtle lay stranded on the beach,
Its shell a mixture of colours.
Ancient secrets hidden within the turtle's mind,
He just lay there waiting.
The water swept onto the beach.
The turtle continued his journey and left,
The secrets went with it.

Joshua Burkmar (10)
Ashford CE Primary School

Colours

Red snow, white apples,
Orange juice with bits,
Yellow sun is hot,
Green grape wine with apple and pine,
Blue flower slime oh how kind.
Indigo pots with something on top,
Violet clocks with big brown dots.

Rebecca Horton (8)
Ashford CE Primary School

My Rainbow Poem

Red is a rose
Shining, glittering after rain,
Orange is a fruit
Juicy and delicious,
Yellow is the sun
Glistening and sparkling,
Blue is the sky,
And so is a bluebird,
Indigo is a sunset,
Changing colour in the evening,
Violet is a flower,
Fluttering in the breeze!

Lauren Nichols (8)
Ashford CE Primary School

Opposites

Black and white are the colours that I like,
It is very bad to be sad but when I am happy, I feel glad,
Down is low and up is high,
Light is bright and dark, I can't even see the park,
Sun and moon I love to see them glow,
I love the day because I can play, and night is where
I lay my head,
Hot and cold is fine either way.

Megan Kyri (10)
Ashford CE Primary School

My Rainbow Poem

Red my favourite colour shining like the sun,
Orange colour of sunset, beauty of all beauties,
Yellow colour of sun, colour of summer,
Green is a frog, green is grass,
Blue colour of the sky, like the Chelsea top,
Indigo a wonderful colour for fish,
Violet a lovely colour for a flower.

Daniel Moore (8)
Ashford CE Primary School

My Rainbow Poem

Red is a rose as wet as when the raindrops have fallen,
Orange is a fruit, tasty and juicy,
Yellow is the sun when everyone's happy,
Green is the grass when it has been watered,
Blue is the sky and all of the sea,
Indigo is a peacock's feather as it shows its property,
Violet is a flower that is beautiful and bright.

Thomas McVey (8)
Ashford CE Primary School

My Rainbow Poem

Red is a rose, shining after the rain,
Orange is an orange,
Yellow is a sun, lovely and bright,
Green is a cucumber, you can eat it,
Blue is a paint, so you can colour your walls,
Indigo is a class, Year 2 in the lower school,
Violet is a nail varnish, you can put it on your nails.

Samantha Leeman (7)
Ashford CE Primary School

My Rainbow Poem

Red is a rose, so shiny when it is raining,
Orange is a fruit, delicious in every way,
Yellow is a sun, very bright in the day,
Green is the grass, dewy when it rains,
Blue is my bedroom, and my favourite colour,
Indigo was my class, in the lower school,
Violet is when the sunset comes and goes when it's night-time.

Daniel Smith (8)
Ashford CE Primary School

My Rainbow Poem

Red is the shining sun, flowers are growing,
Orange is a juicy fruit and a bright colour,
Yellow is the soft sand and the team Mann.
Green is the grass and a slimy frog,
Blue is the sky and a football team's kit,
Indigo is my bedroom and my bed,
Violet is inside a peacock's feather.

Gemma Srnecz (7)
Ashford CE Primary School

My Rainbow Poem

Red is the sunset as red as roses,
Orange is a fruit, sweet and juicy,
Yellow is a colour, as bright as can be,
Green is the grass, muddy after rain,
Blue is the sky, with clouds floating swiftly,
Indigo was a class, warm and cosy,
Violet is a dark sign of bad weather.

David Jacob (7)
Ashford CE Primary School

My Rainbow Poem

Red is a chair, people sit on it,
Orange is a piece of paper, you can use for writing and sums,
Yellow is the sun, and a pen to colour with,
Green is the grass, the leaves and trees,
Blue is the sky and the sea,
Indigo is a classroom in the lower school,
Violet is my bedroom, I have a violet TV!

Charlotte Salisbury (7)
Ashford CE Primary School

My Rainbow Poem

Red is the sun, hot as lard,
Orange is a fruit, tasty and delicious,
Yellow is my pencil writing this poem,
Green is a frog, hopping and jumping,
Blue is sea, smooth and wavy,
Indigo is ink ready to write,
Violet is a flower,
Delicious to smell.

Alex Gasson (7)
Ashford CE Primary School

My Rainbow Poem

Red is a rose, a kind of nice smell,
Orange is a fruit, very juicy and sweet,
Yellow is a sun, a very bright colour,
Green is grass, leaves in the spring,
Blue is a sky, just like a pencil pot,
Indigo is my bedroom cosy and warm,
Violet is a butterfly gently swaying.

Owen Wheeler (8)
Ashford CE Primary School

My Rainbow Poem

Red is a rose, shimmering in the dew,
Orange is a fruit, yummy, juicy dribbling down my chin,
Yellow is the sun, so warm it sometimes burns my skin,
Green is the grass, muddy after rain,
Blue is the sea, as blue as blue can be,
Indigo was my class in the lower school, I liked it a lot,
Violet is the colour of the sunset, beautiful, changing every second.

Ellie Usher (7)
Ashford CE Primary School

My Rainbow Poem

Red is the sun, hot as lava,
Orange is fruit, tasty and delicious,
Yellow is my pencil, writing this poem,
Green is a frog, leap, jump, hop,
Blue is sky full of clouds,
Indigo is ink ready to use,
Violet is a flower, delicious to smell.

Jack Ellingham (7)
Ashford CE Primary School

My Rainbow Poem

Red is a rose, shining in the sun at noon,
Orange is a fruit, juicy and delicious,
Yellow is the sun and a banana,
Green is the grass and so is a tree,
Blue is the sky and so is your eye,
Indigo is a flower and so is a butterfly,
Violet is my bedroom and so are my walls.

Ellen Davis (8)
Ashford CE Primary School

My Rainbow Poem

Red is a rose, fluttering in the breeze,
Orange is a fruit, lovely and juicy,
Yellow is a sun, sizzling at noon,
Green is the grass, that looks like jewels gleaming,
Blue is the sea, shining like crystals,
Indigo is a peacock's feather, gently swaying,
Violet is a purplish shell water flowing through
When the tide is in.

Tom Bulshaw (7)
Ashford CE Primary School

My Rainbow Poem

Red is like a rose, glittering in the sun,
Orange is a fruit, that is delicious,
Yellow is the sun, that shines,
Green is a leaf, that grows on a tree,
Blue is the sea, that the waves go past,
Indigo is my bedroom, that is pretty and safe,
That everyone one looks at.

Hanna Chaudhry-Green (8)
Ashford CE Primary School

My Rainbow Poem

Red is the sun, hot as lava,
Orange is a fruit, tasty and delicious,
Yellow is my pencil, writing this poem,
Green is a frog, jump, hop, leap,
Blue is sky full of clouds,
Indigo is ink, ready to write with,
Violet is a flower, delicious to smell.

Callum Bond (7)
Ashford CE Primary School

My Rainbow Poem

Red is a beautiful rose,
Orange is a juicy fruit,
Yellow is the sun,
Green is for the grass,
Blue is for the sky,
Indigo is ink, dark and wet,
Violet is a flower, fluttering in the breeze.

Charlotte Avis-Winter (7)
Ashford CE Primary School

My Rainbow Poem

Red is the sun, hot as lava,
Orange is fruit, tasty and delicious,
Yellow is my pencil, writing this poem,
Green is a frog, jump, hop, leap,
Blue is sea, smooth or wavy,
Indigo is ink, ready to write,
Violet is a flower, delicious to smell.

Daniel Chamberlain (7)
Ashford CE Primary School

My Rainbow Poem

Red is the sun, hot as lava,
Orange is a fruit, tasty and delicious,
Yellow is my pencil writing this poem,
Green frog, jump, leap, hop,
Blue is sea, smooth,
Indigo ink, ready to write,
Violet is a flower, delicious to smell.

Luke Bagnell (7)
Ashford CE Primary School

My Rainbow Poem

Roses are red, pink in the sun,
Orange is a fruit, mmm juicy!
Yellow is the sun, as bright as can be,
Green is the grass, going whoosh in the wind,
Blue is the sea, just for you and for me,
Indigo is hiding in a peacock's feather,
Showing off in the sunny weather,
Violet is the colour of my room, my clock,
My bed and my broom!

Lucy Gannon (8)
Ashford CE Primary School

My Rainbow Poem

Red is a smelly rose,
Orange is a juicy fruit,
Yellow is beautiful like the sun,
Green is a coloured pencil,
Blue is the sky,
Indigo is a class in lower school,
Violet is just like purple.

Lauren Reeves (8)
Ashford CE Primary School

Sleepover

Sleep around friends,
PlayStation,
McDonald's,
Camp bed,
Sleep!

Jordan Jennings (7)
Ashford CE Primary School

School Poem

I love PE
We do all sorts of things,
Jumping, catching, rounders
And lots more.

Comfy white trainers are what I like to wear,
Itchy and scratchy are the plimsolls that I tear.

When it rains,
We squash into the hall,
I love the sun,
When we go for a run.

We play stuck and rugby, running
And lots more,
But when it rains,
It is not the best,
We stay in and have a rest.

A netball game is really great,
Especially with a best mate.

Charlotte Ross (11)
Ashford CE Primary School

Limerick

There once was a horrible man,
Who ate a great big old can,
He tried and he tried,
But suddenly died,
And then he was thrown in a van.

April Cousins (8)
Ashford CE Primary School

London's Destruction

It's really sad being alone,
An incendiary bomb just fell!
I went outside and there was
A broken rotten bone.
I couldn't stand up,
I just fell!

My candle I lit myself for my own room,
My teddy, so green like an elf,
Suddenly everything went boom!

'Help! Help' said someone,
I rushed downstairs,
There I saw a little one,
I couldn't let him die
It wasn't fair!

A loud cacophony,
Entered my room
Oh no!
Everything went *boom!*

Thamina Miah (10)
Crane Park Primary School

World War II

Today they declared the war,
It was a great devastation!
There was a major evacuation,
When I looked out the door.
You will not believe what I saw,
It was worse than execution.
Will this be the end of our nation?
I don't think I can stand it anymore.
I don't want to live in a war zone!
I want to cry,
Bombs drop from the sky,
What is happening to our home?
When is this war going to end?
It is driving me round the bend!

Bryoni Bowers (11)
Crane Park Primary School

Snow Tiger

Night-creeper,
Forest-sleeper,
Stream-drinker,
Prowling-speaker,
Deer-ripper,
Lake-dipper,
Angry-roarer,
Loud-snorer,
Prey-chaser,
Meal-racer.
What am I?

Abigail Pearce (10)
Echelford Primary School

Zoo

In exhibit 1 there is an animal as orange
As the sun with a neck like a crane.
In exhibit 2 there is an animal as grey
As the pavement with a trunk as long as a snake.
In exhibit 3 there is a cheeky animal that is brown
As chocolate and swings from tree to tree.
In exhibit 4 there is an animal that is black and white
Like a newspaper, a big, furry bear.
In exhibit 5 there is an animal that laughs
Every second of the day, black with sharp white teeth.
In exhibit 6 there is the king of the jungle
As orange as sand and a man as brown as a tree trunk.
In exhibit 7 there is an animal with a white fuzzy tummy
He walks like he has a limp and he has orange webbed feet.
In exhibit 8 I saw a familiar, face starting back at me.
I saw my brother!

Samantha Collins (10)
Echelford Primary School

Kennings Poem

Slimy walker,
Quiet-talker,
Ground-slitherer,
Tongue-flicker,
Good-catcher,
Bad-scratcher,
Sand-trailer,
Bad-failure,
Rubbish-sleeper,
Mice-eater.

What am I?

Mikey Bishay (10)
Echelford Primary School

Hedgehog

A hedgehog is a giant pin cushion,
For the Gods of Mount Olympus,
He is the fear of worms and snails,
And a better berry picker than all.
He is a mechanical infantry,
Able to defend himself from all but dreaded humans,
By rolling into a mace.
He is like my hand creeping along a desk,
Stealthily and silent as a spy.
By the worms . . .
Winter is known as the safe season.

So when you discover at the back of the garden,
A hedgehog sleeping sound,
Do not disturb the horse-chestnut shell,
Covered in crisp leaves, they wouldn't harm you,
So why harm them
As they sleep in the gentle breeze?

Philip Legg (11)
Echelford Primary School

Mouse-Eater

High-flyer,
Egg-hatchers,
Fish-grabber,
Nest-maker,
Egg-dropper,
Mountain-soarer,
Tree-raider,
Fierce-hunter,
Roaming-glider.

What am I?

Jasmine Parsons (11)
Echelford Primary School

Wanted!

Someone is needed who can:
Wash the dishes, scrub the floors,
Clean the clothes and household chores.

A person is required who will:
Be a taxi driver at the drop of a hat,
Join in games - some with a ball or bat.

A teacher is needed who can:
Help with projects and test with spellings,
Solve maths problems and enjoy storytelling.

A carer is required who will:
Be a nursemaid day and night,
Be able to sort out a squabble or a fight.

This position has now been filled,
The contract has been signed and sealed,
There may be many applicants for the post,
But the award will go to the one that loves me most . . .
    My mum!

Abigail Pearce (10)
Echelford Primary School

The Rabbit

Carrot-cruncher,
Claw-scratcher,
Fur-licker,
Nose-twitcher,
Straw-nibbler,
Bouncy-hopper,
Hole-digger.

What am I?

Sam Culverhouse (11)
Echelford Primary School

Hamster

Slow walker,
Food eater,
Finger wibbler,
Furry wanderer,
Wheel turner,
House sleeper,
Tunnel hider,
Hand cuddler,
Sawdust flicker,
Water drinker,
Straw nestler,
Ball runner.

What am I?

Courtney Hatt (10)
Echelford Primary School

Mouse

Cheese-eater,
Ear-scratcher,
Tail-wagger,
Hole-keeper,
Crumb-smeller,
Back-itcher,
Elephant-scarer,
Good-hider.

What am I?

Ashlie Jones (10)
Echelford Primary School

Sidney

Sidney is a bushy fox,
He also is a fierce fox
And his fur is as red as blood,
His teeth are sharper than ten saws.

Once he went to a farm and went to poach a chicken,
When he went the farmer saw him,
And Sidney fell down a trap,
By the next night, he had wriggled free.

Another time he went after a rabbit
With a hunter chasing him with a gun.
Sidney went down a burrow,
And ripped up a rabbit underground.

The next day a gun went *bang,*
And Sidney was the target.
He ran and ran into a pond,
Then he came out and went to his den.

Sidney is a bushy fox,
He also is a fierce fox
And his fur is as red as blood,
His teeth are sharper than ten saws.

Sarah Taplin (10)
Echelford Primary School

The Beach

The sea, is a shimmering diamond,
The sea, is a mammoth warm swimming pool.

The sand, is an immense puddle of yellow rain,
The sand, is a huge sponge.

The sun, is a gigantic orange sphere,
The sun is a considerable ball of fierce fire.

Siân-Louise Thomas (10)
Echelford Primary School

Why Don't They Stop?

Bins on fire,
Litter on streets,
Phone boxes smashed,
Nowhere to meet,
Why don't they stop?

Blinding smoke,
Stenching smell
Polluting the air,
No one to tell,
Why don't they stop?

Rivers polluted with
Rubbish and trash.
When the police come,
They run, they dash.

Chloé Holman (8)
Echelford Primary School

A Ghost

A ghost is a translucent cloud,
A ghost is a howling warrior,
A ghost is a white ocean,
A ghost is a startling nightmare,
A ghost is a spine-chilling beast,
A ghost is a mouth trembling hypnotiser,
A ghost is a demon ascending from Hell!

Emma O'Shea (10)
Echelford Primary School

It's Your Responsibility

Broken ruler's on the floor, pick it up,
It's the law.

Sickening liquids in the lake,
Hold on a minute.
There must be a mistake.

Blinding fumes in the sky.
That's why all the birds are beginning to die.

People throwing rubbish on the floor.
Don't they know what bins are for?

Broken rulers,
Sickening liquids,
Blinding fumes,
Throwing rubbish,
It's everywhere.

Megan Daniels (8)
Echelford Primary School

Shark

Fish-eater,
Fast-swimmer,
Man-catcher,
Blood-eater,
Fast-racer,
Fish-catcher,
Fin-frightener.

What am I?

Jack Knight (10)
Echelford Primary School

Rats

Night-creeper,
Loud-squealer,
Fast-runner,
Rubbish-eater,
Bin-sleeper,
Sly-nipper,
Vicious-biter,
House-intruder,
Vermin-member.

What am I?

Lucy-Simone Short (11)
Echelford Primary School

Spider

Bug eater,
Fly beater,
Ceiling sneaker,
Dark seeker,
Food binder,
Corner finder,
Pattern stunner,
Wall runner,
Web maker,
Life taker.

Alex Pearce-Kelly (10)
Echelford Primary School

Mouse

Cheese-taker,
Squeak-maker,
Fast-runner,
Face-stunner,
Cheese-nibbler,
Fast-dribbler,
Nose-scratcher,
Cheddar-snatcher,
Elephant-scarer,
Paper-tearer.
What am I?

Mel West (11)
Echelford Primary School

Turtle

Shy talker,
slow mover,
lettuce muncher,
hare beater,
winter hibernator,
hard cover,
sleep lover,
house hider.
What am I?

Rosie Kelly (10)
Echelford Primary School

The Magic Box

(Based on 'Magic box' by Kit Wright)

I will put in my box . . .
A furry, fluffy fox fishing for a fish,
The feeling of bubbling bubbles in a warm bath,
An everlasting extraordinary elephant who's
Excellent at tricks.

I will put in my box . . .
A mouse chasing a cat,
A sky of bright purple,
A snake with feet,
A dolphin with hands.

I will put in my box . . .
The first word of a baby,
The sound of a rumbling belly,
A taste of smooth, thick chocolate.

I will put in my box . . .
The smell of fresh lavender,
The sight of a rabbit in a field,
The roughness of a crocodile's skin.

My box is created with
Silver, glittery stars,
A moon of bright cream,
A planet hovering.

I will act in my box,
A play of great enjoyment,
Brilliant excitement,
Then finish with a show of clapping hands.

Eleanor Shaw (10)
Echelford Primary School

Sidney

Sidney was an elaborate elephant,
He often lay by the pool,
Lifted his trunk high in the air,
Taller than them all.

Sidney was an excited elephant,
Who liked to have some fun,
Shame he could not run around,
He weighed half a ton.

Sidney was an efficient elephant,
He was always very clean,
His house was like an ocean,
He was so very keen.

Sidney was an external elephant,
He'd be fun for ever,
You'd spot him out,
He was a potential adventurer.

Sidney was an enterprising elephant,
He started to poach,
The only problem was transport,
'Never mind, I'll take the coach!'

Sidney was an enriched elephant,
For shooting birds down,
He was the champion of the world,
He wanted to wear a crown.

Sidney was an enthusiastic elephant,
But had the longest way to fall,
He wasn't very good that day,
His eyes were watering and he was ready to bawl.

Sidney was an exceeded elephant,
Never did he play again,
His body was all aching,
He was really feeling the pain.

William MacDonald (10)
Echelford Primary School

The Park Last Week

I went to the park last week,
And this is what I found,
The flowers were smelling so sweet,
The ducks were having something to eat.

I went to the park last week,
And this is what I found,
Fluorescent flowers in the flower bed,
Butterflies flying,
Bees buzzing.

I went to the park today,
And this is what I saw,
Graffiti on the swings and slides,
Bins on fire.

I went to the park today,
And this is what I saw
A stench in the air
And rubbish on the bench,
They don't care.

I want them to stop,
They're destroying our environment,
Why do they do it?
It's not fair!

Because you know what
The most dangerous creature in the world is . . .
You, me, everyone!

Katherine Church (9)
Echelford Primary School

Graffiti

I look out of the train window
And what do I see?
A lot of graffiti and no trees.

I look out of the car window
And what do I see?
A smashed up phone box and a heap of dry leaves.

I look out of the boat window
And what do I see?
Old cigarettes floating on the sea.

I look out of the bus window
And what do I see?
Teenage people covering the walls with graffiti.

I look out of the plane window
And what do I see?
A cloud of fumes and no sparkling sea.

I look out of my bedroom window
And what do I see?
November 5th's fireworks in the night-black sky.

Emily Karlsson (8)
Echelford Primary School

Horse

A horse is a galloping rage of speed,
Running across the field as fast as a cheetah,
Trotting, slowly and gracefully,
Ride on the horse and gallop across the field,
Silky and shiny fur in the sun,
A horse is a fast car running across the road,
His mane is a flag in the wind.

Neil Harrold (10)
Echelford Primary School

Vandalism

They've destroyed and ruined the river,
So you can hardly see it!
But why did they?
Who knows?

They don't use the dump,
They throw it in the countryside,
But why have they done it?
No one knows.

They've spoilt the views
By wrecking our world,
But how can they do it?
I don't know.

Maybe for fun,
Because they don't care,
But why don't they stop?
We don't know.

They are me,
They are you,
They're our family,
They're The Queen,
They're the government,
They're the factories,
That's who does it.

Claire Scott
Echelford Primary School

Vile Vandalism

Why do they do it?
I don't know.
They don't care.
They poison most things anywhere.
They don't care.

Why do they do it?
I don't know.
They think they're ace.
They're really a disgrace.
They don't care!

Why do they do it?
I don't know.
They spoil the environment,
Change the best views,
And they're really rude.
They don't care!

Why do they do it?
I don't know.
Broken property, call the police.
A teenager broke a lamp post
With a hammer which I've seen.
Because they don't care!

Christian Bonning (8)
Echelford Primary School

Volcano

A volcano is a steaming bowl of soup being knocked out of
someone's hand,
A volcano is an exploding bottle of Fanta Fruit Twist,
A volcano is a cup of cherryade being poured over the floor,
A volcano is somebody's blood gushing out after being shot
several times,
A volcano is a punnet of strawberries being sat on by an elephant,
A volcano is a house on fire spreading down the street.

Joshua Hankin (11)
Echelford Primary School

At The Park

Why do they do it?
I don't know,
Throwing rubbish in the park.

Why do they do it?
I don't know,
Shattered glass bottles against the park wall.

Why do they do it?
I don't know,
Stench of old food all over the park.

Why do they do it?
I don't know.

Sophie Allaway (8)
Echelford Primary School

The T-Rex

How small unto the giant T-rex
Must big things look,
Trees like broccoli
That shook and shook.

The sun, a tennis ball,
A blackboard like a book,
A sparkling moon up in the sky
Like a diamond taken by a crook.

Ricky Fryer (8)
Echelford Primary School

The Bull

How small unto the brave bull
Must big things look,
A palm tree like broccoli,
The palm tree shuddered and shook.

The sun like a tennis ball,
The clouds like cotton wool,
The shiny stars like glistening sparklers,
The world is never dull.

The moon like a light bulb,
Planet Mars like fire,
A flowing river, a little stream,
Frothy white pollution like cream.

Giorgia Clark (9)
Echelford Primary School

Graffiti

More dazzling than the sun,
More beautiful than a sunset,
Do you know what it is?
Graffiti!

More colourful than the rainbow,
More blinding than the eclipse,
Do you know what it is?
Graffiti!

Shimmering silver and fluorescent yellow,
Aqua-blue and ruby-red,
Do you know what it is?
Graffiti!

Cameron McCoig (9)
Echelford Primary School

Graffiti

Spiralling showers cover the wall
Improving the enjoyment,
More blinding than the sun,
It's graffiti!

Fluorescent flowers cover the wall,
More colours than the rainbow,
It's graffiti!

Skull-white and blood-red.
Improving the environment,
It's graffiti!

Fluorescent tornados of colour
Turquoise-blue, glittering gold,
Shimmering silver,
It's graffiti!

Karim Bhaluani (9)
Echelford Primary School

Who Am I?

A fuzzy ball waiting to attack?
A fearsome warrior?
A cute, cuddly monster?
A wall of eyes?
A tiger with gleaming eyes?
A lion with his handsome mane?
A cheetah, faster than light?
A panther purring proudly?
A puma prancing?
    No! A kitten.

Gareth Davey (10)
Echelford Primary School

The Dressing Up Box

In the dressing up box there is . . .
A fancy lacy dress with big, floppy shoes,
A hat with flowers,
That's never been used!

In the dressing up box there is . . .
Mum's old tatty skirts,
Gran's gold sandals,
Dad's holey jumper that he got from Uncle Bert!

In the dressing up box there is . . .
Gran's worn out blanket with an old-fashioned watch,
Mum's shabby wedding hat,
Grandad's red tie covered in blue spots!

In the dressing up box there is . . .
Sister Louise's old ballet dress with the matching shoes,
Unused clown bow ties
That used to give Mum terrible blues!

In the dressing up box there is . . .
Baby Jessica's old bonnets with painted shirts,
Loads of handbags,
Some things my sister should wear, *flirt!*

In the dressing up box there is . . .
Aunt Ruby's fake earrings and some manky jumpers,
Baked bean tops,
And an old bag with an ancient compass!

A flowery pair of jeans,
And slippers upon slippers that need a good sort.

In the dressing up box there is . . .
Uncle Tom's top hat surrounded by my old Brownie clothes,
Some fairy wings,
Danger! Danger! of being suffocated by Dad's old socks!

Jessica Pryor (11)
Echelford Primary School

What's Behind The School Stage?

What's behind the school stage?
A family of giant spiders
Who are such very good climbers,
Well, I'm not going to see.

What's behind the school stage?
A one-eyed man
With his frying pan,
Well, I'm not going to see.

What's behind the school stage?
Seven dead people
Who haunted a church steeple,
Well, I'm not going to see.

What's behind the school stage?
A headless ghost
Who used to boast,
Well, I'm not going to see.

What's behind the school stage?
Eleven ghost riders
Who are friends of spiders,
Well, I'm not going to see.

What's behind the school stage?
A vampire from a church spire
Who used to be the town crier,
Well, I'm not going to see.

Adam Huse (11)
Echelford Primary School

My Big Brother

He's a money-taker,
He's a bruise-maker,
He's a game-nicker,
He's a hard kicker.
He's a powerful puncher,
He's a bone-cruncher,
He's a curfew-breaker,
He hurts me later.
He's a room messer,
He's an expensive dresser,
He's a bad driver,
He owes me a fiver,
He's a terrible brother,
I want another.

Dominic Hadi (11)
Echelford Primary School

A Crocodile

A crocodile's skin is a green log that kills,
Its blood is red fire,
Its teeth are sharp daggers that dig into your skin,
Its jaws are two planks that slam together,
Its tail is a strong whip that whips enemies,
Its eyes are balls of fire,
It body is very, very strong,
So *watch ooouuuttt!*

Jessica Beagley (10)
Echelford Primary School

The Magic Box

(Based on 'Magic Box' by Kit Wright)

I will put in my box . . .
A glimpse of a glittering garden in the winter,
The smell of hot apple pie on a cold night,
The taste of warm chocolate melting upon my lips.

I will put in my box . . .
The touch of cold snow in the winter,
A soothing whisper of my mum when I am ill,
The dazzling colours of a fluorescent fish.

I will put in my box . . .
More colours than the rainbow,
The sound of the waves on the beach,
The touch of a smooth dolphin.

I will put in my box . . .
The thirteenth month and a blue apple,
An old lady with a dummy,
And a baby with a glass of champagne.

I will surf in my box,
The waves of sunny Cornwall,
And play on the beach,
Eating cold vanilla ice cream.

Laura Butler (10)
Echelford Primary School

Elephants

An elephant is a water pistol squirting everyone,
A huge boulder rolling down a sandy hill,
The tail is a long snake hanging from a tree, swaying from side to side,
Their beady eyes are little black pebbles,
The foot is a huge drum banging on the ground,
An elephant's legs are tree stumps,
It is a trumpet being blown non-stop,
Its ears are flags flowing in the wind.

Laura Turner (10)
Echelford Primary School

The Magic Box

(Based on 'Magic Box' by Kit Wright)

I will put in my box . . .
The silent sound of slithering snakes,
A 32nd day in a month,
And cats crawling quietly in the night sky.

I will put in my box . . .
The sight of leaves falling,
The taste of chocolate melting on my lips,
The touch of a newborn animal with no fur or feathers.

I will put in my box . . .
The smell of dinner,
The sounds of birds singing,
And snow in winter, cold and icy.

I will put in my box . . .
A 30th day in February.
The sounds of birds talking
And humans tweet-tweeting.

My box is decorated with
Diamonds and gems, and as hinges
It has skeletons' knuckles.

I will play in my box . . .
With the newborn animals,
And build a whole town with houses and buses.
That's what I'll put in my box.

Samantha Curtis (9)
Echelford Primary School

Get Rid Of War

We should all be peaceful,
We should all learn to love,
We should see the people around us
And take a look above.

We should see the sky
Turning from blue to grey,
Filling with bullets and bombs,
People are running away.

The war has started,
And people are dying,
We can hear the gunshots,
But there is no peace flying.

All the innocent creatures
Are lying dead on the ground,
And there are lots of people
Screaming all around.

If there had been peace,
It would be more like this:
People would laugh and play,
Not mourning for people they miss.

Peace and unity are the answer,
That is for sure,
If people just got along,
There wouldn't be war anymore.

So for you people in the future,
Read this poem and stop
To think if war is such a good idea,
Because I think it's a flop!

Haider Hussain (7)
Edgware Junior School

I Have A Big Bogey

I look in the mirror one chilly afternoon,
I see a big bogey the size of a moon,
I yell and I sniff
I pull and I lift,
It won't come out
So I yell and I shout.
It is bright yellow and green,
I cannot be seen.
I wish and wish for it to go,
But it won't leave my nose, you know.
When I go out there's always trouble,
If I have a bogey, it will be double.
What can I do? There is nowhere to run,
Picking a bogey just isn't fun.
It's rude and it's gross,
I refuse to pick my nose.
Um,
Shall I pick it? Shall I not?
I do not, I've picked a spot.
Here it goes, I'm going to pick it,
Oops, I flicked it.
There it goes on my dad's plate,
Oh no, my bogey's been ate!

Holly Watkins (11)
Edgware Junior School

Cyclone Poem

The
roaring
thunderous
screeching
cyclone
monster
destroys
everything
in
seconds.
Before
you
can
even
think
about
it
it
just
comes
and
eats
you.
Revolting
isn't
it?
If
you
are
afraid
run away
like a scaredy-cat.

George Kust (9)
Edgware Junior School

The Santa Secret

It isn't known across the world
By any mum or dad
That for 364 days
Santa's really bad

His bedroom's so untidy
He never eats his greens
And underneath his big red suit
He never ever cleans

He never likes to blow his nose
And will not wipe his feet
He does not use his knife and fork
When it's time to eat

So if you're ever told at all
That Santa won't come if you're bad
Don't believe a word of this
From any mum or dad.

Shona Dann (9)
Edgware Junior School

Why?

Sometimes I wonder why
why God made a big blue sky.

I wonder why he made the night
and why people choose to fight.

I wonder why trees are green
and why some people are so mean.

Why can't the people come together,
wind or rain whatever the weather.

Why can't they join hands like a piece of lace,
the world would be a better place.

I wonder why God made me,
I think the world was meant to be.

Ellesha Howell (11)
Edgware Junior School

Things That Should Be Done

Dirty clothes should be put in the hamper,
Clean clothes should be put in the drawer,
But it takes too much time and it takes too much work,
So I just throw it all on the floor!

Toys should be put in the toy box,
Covers be straight on my bed,
Books should be neat on the bookshelf
And garden tools in the shed!
But it takes too much time and it takes too much work,
So I just watch TV instead!

Mum says I'm messy
Never do as I'm told
My room is a pigsty,
My things growing mould!

I don't care what she says
She drives me berserk
So I just don't respond
I don't *like* too much work!

Tara Bush (10)
Edgware Junior School

Arsenal FC

A shley Cole and Thierry Henry,
R obert Pires and Patrick Viera.
S eaman's the keeper that left,
E du and Gilberto.
N aughty Keown and Dennis Bergkamp,
A rsene Wenger is the manager.
L jungberg and Sol Campbell,

F or Arsenal are the best football
C lub in the world, to me and my mates.

Youssef Djeraoui (11)
Edgware Junior School

The Cyclone

Here comes a dark cyclone
Bang! Bang! Bang!
It's hungry, it's mad
It's noisy, it's a cyclone
Bang! Bang! Bang!
Here comes the cyclone
Whirling, twirling
Roar! Roar! Roar!
Bang!
Here comes the cyclone
Ravenous, curling, gobbling
Bang! Bang! Roar!

Kessia Destifanis (8)
Edgware Junior School

My Type Of Dog

Her lips as red as rosy cheeks
Her fur as golden as a ring
Her muzzle as black as Black Beauty
Her feet as white as snow
Her eyes as brown as a tree
Her tongue as pink as cherry bubblegum
Now that's my type of dog.

Robert Stevens (9)
Edgware Junior School

Orlando

I love going to Orlando we all have lots of fun there,
Whatever we do, I have fun so I don't care.
I love going to Orlando on the plane,
Because we get to watch TV and play games.
I love having our own villa, we get to have our own pool,
So when it is really hot we can stay nice and cool.
I love going to the beach because there are lots of things to do,
Like playing in the sand or whatever you want to.
I love going to the theme parks and going on lots of rides,
There are so many to choose from I can't believe my eyes.
I love going shopping, we all buy a lot,
I love having meals in restaurants because
What I want they have got.

Jodie Cottol (10)
Edgware Junior School

The Dancing Fish

She used to dance under the shiny, sparkly water,
Down and up without any toil at all.
Who taught her how to swim?
Under the waves while she twirls and spins.
Don't catch her and make her into a show.
Oh how beautiful she is, this fish.
Look at her dancing happily.
Swimming with laughter,
Saving the people who are nearly dead.
Let's go with her, singing and dancing.
She is the *dolphin fish*.

Nosaiba Drera (10)
Edgware Junior School

My Class

Some of us are sneaky
the rest of us cheeky

Some of us are horrid
some are very torrid

Some of us are good
the rest really should

Some of us are really bright
the rest of us need to turn on the light

This is my class they're in a state
but then my teacher is really great.

Ceri Ellis (10)
Edgware Junior School

The Cake Poem

I love cakes they're so yummy in my tummy
The smell of strawberries I love the best
I could eat all of them
I love cakes so much that I could smell them from miles away.
It's just a shame they're all gone
I ate them all so that's a big shame
But when I go to Africa I can eat all the cakes there, yummy, yummy
I love cakes they're so yummy in my tummy.

Keeley Don (8)
Edgware Junior School

The Dog Of Doom

In a faraway kennel,
There lives a dog,
He's as daft as a dunce,
He's as dumb as a doorknob.

He calls himself the Dog of Doom,
He thinks he is clever,
Neither are true, as he also thinks,
He is the fastest dog in the world.

He couldn't run without help,
But it is not surprising,
Because he is as I said,
As daft as a dunce
And as dumb as a doorknob.

Jordan Turner (9)
Edgware Junior School

Strange Cats

My cat's blue just like you.
My cat's yellow, yellow like the sunshine.
My cat's red, dark as a devil.
My cat's black and furry.
Your one's too blurry.
My one's too itchy.
We've all got strange cats.
Different colours
And funny things happen to them.

Farva Baqir (8)
Edgware Junior School

Nine Things I Found In A Giant's Pocket

Underpants the size of King Kong
and red socks that really pong.
A toilet that can talk and fly like a hawk
and a pen the size of a chilli.

An eye the size of a football
a football the size of an eye.
Ten children locked in a cage
all dying of rage and going on the rampage.

A fluff ball the size of a bed
and a dragon's head
this is what I found in a giant's pocket.

Spencer Mogge & Callum Woodbridge (9)
Holy Trinity CE Primary School

Homeless

I feel sorry for some people,
No money, no food,
No friends, no family, no one that cares,
Just a few coins,
Nothing much more,
Nowhere to go,
No home, no front door.

Oliver Matthews (9)
Holy Trinity CE Primary School

Overheard On A Salt Marsh

'Angel, angel what are your emeralds?'
'Great Fawn why do you look at them?'
'Give them.'
'No!'
'Then I will ram the trees with anger.
I will do it with all my strength.'
'Fawn, why are they precious to you?'
'They are better than a warm sunset,
Better than any fair gold ring
Better than any shining star
They are better than life itself.'
'Give them to me.'
'Never.'
'Let me have the emeralds.
I will treasure them for life,
I will love them so.
Give me, give them to me, give them.'
'No, no, no.'

Ben Jones (9)
Holy Trinity CE Primary School

What Is That?

'What is that Mother
Floating up there,
That is bluish bright
And stares at me everywhere?'

'That is the sky my wolf son
That covers the Earth
And hides the sun and the moon
That baby animals look at, at their birth.'

Malak Fouda (10)
Holy Trinity CE Primary School

Anita

This is the story of a girl called Anita,
Someday I'll bet you meet 'er,
She's perfect, she's a star,
She's never silly however far.
You won't believe she was once bad,
Oh the trouble we all had,
Oh the shouts, oh the screams,
She was only quiet in her dreams,
She toppled tables,
She toppled chairs,
She pushed the teachers down the stairs,
She got the cane at least six times
And was bad at nine times nine,
But when it came to ghosts and hooties,
She nearly died of ghastly cooties,
'Argh!' she'd scream, what a fright,
In the silent dead of night,
So this gave Mum and Dad a spring,
To sort out this behavioural thing,
Now this is what they had in mind,
To make Anita sweet and kind.
Their plan was slick, their plan was smooth,
For it to work they'd have to move,
See they'll dress up like a freaky beast
And on the kindness they will feast,
So in the cover of the night
They gave Anita such a fright.
'You be perfect no dismay
Or else you'll meet your dying day.'
From this day on she has been,
A perfect girl, a real queen.

Andrew H Johnson (10)
Holy Trinity CE Primary School

Jabbermockery

(Based on 'Jabberwocky' by Lewis Carroll)

'Tis late at night and the furry-tweeters
Squawk and tweet a lot,
I wish that I could shut them up,
But rather loud than not.

Beware the furry-tweeters my friend,
Their claws that grab, their feathers that tickle,
Beware the eagle that pecks alive,
Its deadly feet that prickle.

It took its prey, worm in hand,
Long time they have been doing this,
So tired eagle rested,
With nasty snake that hissed.

'Tis late at night and the furry, feathered friends,
Squawk and tweet a lot,
I wish that I could shut them up,
But rather loud than not.

Jenny Murray (10)
Holy Trinity CE Primary School

Fear

The creaking of the floorboards,
That can only mean one thing.
The flickering of the candlelight,
It must be him.

Fear, you're scaring me,
The way you slither up the door.
The way you crawl with flaming eyes,
Then you shrivel to the floor.

Jade Soiza (10)
Holy Trinity CE Primary School

My Brother Saw An Elephant Circus

My brother saw an elephant circus,
By the greengrocer a day in June,
The master stood with whip and hat
And had a pin that looked like the moon

And Sally the elephant lifted up its head
And lifted up its big feet
And all the children laughed to see
It being whipped in the summer heat.

They watched as it looped and turned,
They watched as it came to a halt.
They heard the master cry with glee,
'Now roly-poly, somersault!'

They paid a dollar for the show
While the master adjusted his cape,
Poor Sally longed to be
In the hot African landscape.

Monica Ashby (10)
Holy Trinity CE Primary School

The World The First Time

'What is that rumbling my mother?
That rumbling that comes from the sky,
Which scares the sun and the creatures
And throws the clouds from the sky?'

'That is the thunder, my wolf son,
The anger of the Earth coming by,
It throws a black cloak over world and sky
And all are afraid of it - all.'

Samara Deng (11)
Holy Trinity CE Primary School

My Jabberwocky

(Based on 'Jabberwocky' by Lewis Carroll)

My jabberwocky is creepy-crawlies,
They creep all over the floor,
They give me huge goose-prawlies,
As they creep up my bedroom door.

Beware the creepy-crawlies my son!
They'll crush you like strawberry jam!
They'll put you in a bun
And eat you like honey roast ham!

The scorpions will get their stings ready,
They'll cut you up and leave you to boil,
They'll be very, very steady,
They'll leave you to cool, then wrap you in foil.

The spiders will creep all over you,
They'll snap like bloodthirsty giants,
They'll shout, *'Boo!'* when they've reached you,
Don't forget, some grow as big as lions.

Harshini Ranchhod (10)
Holy Trinity CE Primary School

Winter

Please don't shiver,
Stop covering my house with snow,
Stop making the whole house cold.
You're freezing everyone to death
And putting ice down on the road isn't funny.
You're making everyone get a chill,
I'm just asking you to stop.

Karina Smith (10)
Holy Trinity CE Primary School

Lights Out

It scares me in the evening,
It scares me in the night.
Every time I try to sleep,
I get a big fright.

I find the darkness creepy,
I get a funny feeling.
Every time I hear a noise,
I look up at the ceiling.

I think I saw something move,
No, it must just be my mind,
Oh no there it is again,
What's it trying to find?

It's crawling over to me,
Maybe I should whisper.
Oh no it's going to get me,
Wait . . . it's just my little sister!

Luke Wilburn (11)
Holy Trinity CE Primary School

Lightning

I find lightning very scary,
Whenever I look out the window,
I have a big fright from behind,
It looks very shiny and bright,
Outside in the cold, cold night,
Fighting its way through the clouds
And the rain.

Hakim Sakaraka (11)
Holy Trinity CE Primary School

Jabbermockery

(Based on 'Jabberwocky' by Lewis Carroll)

'Twas a Saturday night,
the shops were starting to close.
Some people don't think so but
it gives me a fright.

Beware of the lifts my friend
they go up and down.
The sharp jaws open with a yawn
they really do never end!

In go people out come some more
frowning and smiling through the metal door.
Children crying, adults smiling
as they get shaken up once more.

Elise Jones (10)
Holy Trinity CE Primary School

Winter

Don't go rushing all around me,
Stop crying down on me,
Covering everything with snow,
You are not the only one who has problems,
Stop blowing things over.
You are making everything cold,
Stop, stop, stop being so crazy!

Zoe Byrne (11)
Holy Trinity CE Primary School

Jabbermockery

(Based on 'Jabberwocky' by Lewis Carroll)

'Twas Monday night and the bats were out,
hunting their food with all their might.
The cunning foxes were alert for anything that passed.

Beware of the spider creature, who creeps through the darkness,
he stays up high, he stays down low
nobody knows where he will go!

Midnight came, the darkness grew to its highest point.
Everything was silent except a few jabbering sheep.
The foxes were still awake hunting their prey.
Everyone was sleeping it was nearly morning.

So the bats got their meal,
the foxes got their prey,
the spider creature's still in my worst dreams,
the jabbering sheep were now sleeping,
everything was silent as morning grew closer.

Jessica Leigh (11)
Holy Trinity CE Primary School

Autumn

The cold autumn days,
The smell of burning fireworks
Townspeople are gloomy,
As there's no sunlight rays.

While little animals are snoring,
Steaming apple pie is made
And children are using conkers,
For very easy fighting.

Nobody can see in the mist,
Hallowe'en masks are ready,
Time is going backwards
Kids getting told off, don't they get the gist?

Nikhil Chavda (10)
Holy Trinity CE Primary School

Acrostic Poem

S pring, the sun is strong and bright
P rocessing the lovely light
R adishes will grow all in a lovely row
I ce has not come yet
N ice flowers we will never forget
G rowing food and lovely flowers.

S uper summer and sunlight
U nusual flowers, what a delight
M arvellous sun
M agnificent like Turkish Delight
E rasing no sunlight
R unning hot

A utumn comes, no more leaves
U sed conkers, lots of trees
T ired people looking for conkers
U ntied shoelaces, warm inside
M ilkshake drinkers run around
N o more sandcastles, lots of leaves

W hite, thick snow on the ground
I cy icicles, cold as can be
N ice presents all for me
T errified snowman, big and fluffy
E veryone had enough
R eally cold every day.

Dominic Williams (7)
Holy Trinity CE Primary School

Ghost!

It creeps up the hallway,
It hates the break of day.
It climbs up the staircase,
It walks in its steady pace.
It's right by your door,
It's creaking the floor.
It's coming in your room,
It's coming to scare you.
What do you do?
You shout . . . *ghost!*

Will Ashby (10)
Holy Trinity CE Primary School

The Hunting Light

'What is that shining up above, Mother,
That shines in the base of your eye?
Why does it not move in the wind, Mother
And has only half in the sky?'

'That is the moon, my owl son,
It is the king of the night.
Along with the stars it shines
And gives us our hunting light.'

Milly Bowen (11)
Holy Trinity CE Primary School

Acrostic Poem

S unlight pops out of clear skies
P eople start coming outside
R ain stops pouring down
I like the pretty lambs
N ow lots of animals are born
G reat cockerel wakes up at dawn

S un is blazing very bright
U mbrellas for sun are going up
M ost people are paddling in the sea
M y family goes on holiday
E veryone is outside
R ed-hot sun is here

A ll the leaves are falling down
U p from the trees
T he lawn is covered with leaves
U seful rakes are out
M y goodness what a breeze
N ow winter's on its way

W hat has winter done to us?
I t makes us feel so cold
N o one has come outside
T he trees are bare
E very day is darker
R eady for a new year.

Sarah Hunt (7)
Holy Trinity CE Primary School

Acrostic Poem

S mall little lambs are born
P laying in the sun
R ising flowers coming up
I n the spring it's nearly summer
N ow all the colours are here
G oing to be summer

S pring's gone
U p to summer
M ake the holidays be here
M erry summer, merry holidays
E veryone is happy, everyone is glad
R owing, rowing holiday is here

A utumn's back no more summer
U p from the trees you can see the cold
T he people are cold but not frosted yet!
U seful tools to get the leaves out
M orning around causes us all colds
N obody is out of their house

W inter is where Christmas comes
I t's fun to build snowmen
N ow everybody's running round
T rees are bare, nobody is there
E veryone is very cold
R eady for Christmas.

Sally Boultbee (7)
Holy Trinity CE Primary School

Fear

When we're all cosy and snug,
Asleep in our beds,
You sneak up on us
And terrorise our heads.
You make us sweat
And scream and shout,
You laugh at us,
When we writhe about.
Fear, I hate you,
You're as evil as a snake,
You sneak into our minds
And stay until we wake.

Shefali Parmar (11)
Holy Trinity CE Primary School

The Cruncher

'Tis grinning and the people know
That somewhere in the town,
There's a creepy-crawlie
That's skinny and brown.

It stays at night, it hunts at day,
'Beware of the cruncher!'
The people say.

Steffi Lai (10)
Holy Trinity CE Primary School

Acrostic Poem

W hen the weather is cold and shivery
I t means winter is here
N o leaves on the trees
T he animals hibernate
E verybody is wrapped up warm
R ivers frozen and icy

A nimals getting ready for winter
U mbrellas up for rain coming down
T he squirrel is collecting acorns
U p in the trees the birds are singing
M any leaves on the ground
N ights get dark earlier.

Tom Wheatland (7)
Holy Trinity CE Primary School

Friends

Good friends share,
Nasty friends are not fair,
My best friend is always there,
Nasty friends do not care.

My friend says, 'Are you alright?'
Nasty friends say, 'Do you want a fight?'
My friend said, 'No,
In case you might bite!'

My best friend is my best mate,
We get on well and never hate,
We enjoy playing games, having fun,
Playing football, having a run.

Grant Gilbert (11)
Pinkwell Primary School

Conversation

'I've got some perfume,'
'For whom?'
'A girl,'
'I think I'm gonna hurl.'

'When are you going to give it to her?'
'Valentine's Day I think she would prefer.'
'How much was it?'
'Mum gave it to me; Dad thought she was a twit.

Please don't tell anyone.'
'Hmm . . . I might have some fun.'
'Ooi!'
'Can't I even tell Roy?

Will she like it?'
'She'd better or I'll have a fit.'
'I'm sure she will.'
'You're right it's not too big or too lil'.'

'I like it,'
'I'm not giving it to you, you twit.'
'If she doesn't like it can you give it to me?'
'Maybe for a little fee.'

Aron Ahluwalia (10)
Pinkwell Primary School

Springtime

Springtime arrives and hummingbirds sing,
Daffodils grow and bumblebees sting.
Sunny days return and brighten up the sky,
Birds of youth learn how to fly.

Trees begin to blossom, day by day,
A spider's silky web glistens,
By the sun's strong ray.
Rainfalls are rife, during April showers,
Fluffy white clouds sail over beautiful flowers.

Sarika Vashi (10)
Pinkwell Primary School

Volcano

Boiling hot lava
exploding out,
clouds of ash
blocking out the sun,
red river flowing
slowly then fast,
tearing away everything
in its path.
Burning branches
sinking slowly,
engulfed by raging molten rocks.
Deafening roar fills the air
acid squirting
steam flaring,
boiling hot lava oozes out,
scorched landscape
with red, burning liquid
from the murky depths,
spread hot on the ground.
Sulphur smell overpowering,
life blackened and charred,
searing hot river,
taking over,
bubbling and spreading
tearing with revenge
squirting flames, showers of ash,
depositing on ground.
Creatures escaping
the toxic river
of red.

Hafsah Khan (10)
Pinkwell Primary School

Teacher's Pet

On the first day she walked into class,
We all thought she couldn't afford a bus pass,
With the scruffy clothes she had,
She sat down with her bag.

She looked my teacher in the eye,
My teacher exclaimed, 'Ah, there you are sweetie pie
Is Eliza the name?
Oh, my aunt's is the same!'

Eliza who always thought she was wiser,
Became the trouble at school,
She would prance past the boys
Making quite a lot of noise,
As they would comment, 'Wow, she's really cool!'

And whenever she hurt herself,
My teacher was always there to see to her health,
As she would burst into tears and cry.
'Look at that teacher's pet,' I would sigh.

And when we sat in class,
My teacher handed out old homework on mass.
Eliza would show off that she received an 'A',
The class would then bellow, 'No way!'

Looking down at the 'F' on my paper,
I hoped my next piece of homework wouldn't be on water vapour.
I then said with a sigh,
'Teacher's pet, why oh why?'

Priya Kapur (11)
Pinkwell Primary School

SATs

Wake up in the morning feeling tired and sick,
Sit up in my bed, as the clock ticks,
Looking at the calendar,
We're already in May.

Get to school, thinking of SATs,
Look at the board and see double maths,
SATs are as boring as listening to my teacher,
Who, by the way, looks like an ugly creature.

Sitting my maths test,
I'm trying my best,
Trying to work out why, they're so pointless,
As I'd rather listen to my teacher's lectures.

SATs are like a painful death,
Don't do well, then it will be a threat,
Giving my test in,
Why, what'll happen next?
Perhaps a really painful death!

Sonal Bhatt (10)
Pinkwell Primary School

Pop Music

Music - pop, rock and all others,
but my favourite is pop,
from Beyoncé to Big Brovaz
but the best 10 Top.

Quiet, peaceful, loud, mega loud,
have any depending on the mood,
my choice, mega loud,
a cheering crowd.

Come to singers, I go for Sean Paul,
good looking, handsome,
now that's my Sean Paul,
come let's go and listen to classic Rome.

Music, music,
classic music is the best,
you can dance to it and listen to it,
but classic music is always the best.

Aroosa Sheikh (10)
Pinkwell Primary School

Who My Mum Fancies

My mum fancies Jonny Wilkinson
He is very muddy
My mum fancies Jonny Wilkinson
He is fit too
My mum fancies Jonny Wilkinson
He is good at rugby
My mum fancies Jonny Wilkinson
But don't forget about me!

Loren Adkin (7)
Raglan Junior School

When Olivia Say

When Olivia say shrink
yuh better grow

When Olivia say catch
yuh better throw

When Olivia say run
yuh better walk

When Olivia say dumb
yuh better talk

When Olivia say happy
yuh better sad

When Olivia say calm
yuh better mad

When Olivia say go
yuh better stop

When Olivia say open
yuh better lock.

Olivia Watts (8)
Raglan Junior School

When Bradley Say

When Bradley say up
yuh better down

When Bradley say country
yuh better town

When Bradley say on
yuh better off

When Bradley say butterfly
Yuh better moth.

Bradley Phillips (7)
Raglan Junior School

When Oliver Say

When Oliver say crooked
yuh better straight

When Oliver say late
yuh better early

When Oliver say smart
yuh better dumb

When Oliver say run
yuh better walk

When Oliver say awake
yuh better sleep

When Oliver say laugh
yuh better weep.

Oliver Lewis (7)
Raglan Junior School

When Emily Say

When Emily say shhh
yuh better talk

When Emily say run
yuh better walk

When Emily say black
yuh better white

When Emily say draw
yuh better write

When Emily say talk
yuh better yell

When Emily say bad
yuh better be well.

Emily Campion (7)
Raglan Junior School

When Roberto Say

When Roberto say stop
yuh better go

When Roberto say to
yuh better fro

When Roberto say sleep
yuh better awake

When Roberto say fix
yuh better break

When Roberto say lose
yuh better win

When Roberto say drown
yuh better swim

When Roberto say well
yuh better sick

When Roberto say tock
yuh better tick.

Roberto Moscattini (8)
Raglan Junior School

Snow

The snow is as white as wool,
It lays like a big soft blanket.

When I see snow I feel excited,
It feels like a teddy.
The snow is cold but wet
To play in.

I make snowballs and snowmen
With coal and a carrot
And hat, scarf and pipe.

Luke Christodoulou (8)
Raglan Junior School

When Samantha Say

When Samantha say zig
yuh better zag

When Samantha say good
yuh better bad

When Samantha say cold
yuh better warm

When Samantha say dusk
yuh better dawn

When Samantha say tock
yuh better tick

When Samantha say well
yuh better sick

When Samantha say boo
yuh better cheer.

Samantha Whitbread (8)
Raglan Junior School

When Michael Say

When Michael say bye
yuh better hello

When Michael say high
yuh better low

When Michael say asleep
yuh better awake

When Michael say break
yuh better make

When Michael say do
yuh better don't

When Michael say will
yuh better won't.

Michael Rose (7)
Raglan Junior School

When Jessie Say

When Jessie say swim
yuh better drown

When Jessie say smile
yuh better frown

When Jessie say true
yuh better lie

When Jessie say wet
yuh better dry

When Jessie say down
yuh better up

When Jessie say stretch
yuh better tuck.

Jessica Morrison Nicol (7)
Raglan Junior School

Summer

Summer is hot,
Summer is sunshine,
Summer is bright,
Summer is the beach,
Summer means longer days,
Summer is June, July and August,
We love summer, not the rainy days.

Sahel Manuchehry Wahed (7)
Raglan Junior School

Rhyming Ninja Poem

Ninja, Ninja creeping through the night,
Ninja, Ninja come on and fight.
Ninja, Ninja fast asleep,
Ninja, Ninja dressed up as a sheep.
Ninja, Ninja got a mission now,
Ninja, Ninja please show me how.
Ninja, Ninja I've got it,
Ninja, Ninja you've been hit.
Ninja, Ninja double this,
Ninja, Ninja I can wish.
Ninja, Ninja with his sword,
Ninja, Ninja is very bored.
Ninja, Ninja is very good,
Ninja, Ninja has put up his hood.
Ninja, Ninja sleeps in a heap,
Ninja, Ninja has an invisible jeep.
Ninja, Ninja just been hit,
Ninja, Ninja won't quit.

Jack Smith (8)
Raglan Junior School

Aliens And Universe

Aliens are gooey and funny,
Aliens are weird and small.
Spaceships are fast and big.
Planets are big and chunky.
Planets are bigger than monkeys.
Sun is boiling hot.
Stars are small and lonely.

Tom Hassan (7)
Raglan Junior School

How Ellie Became My Best Friend

One day I saw Ellie
Walking up the hill with a pail.
Then she sat down
And examined a snail.

She saw me
And we started to play.
'Meet my sister,' said Ellie,
'Her name is Kay.'

We went to the cafe
And we started to chat.
Soon we felt tired
So we went to Ellie's flat.

Ellie said I could stay
And she said we would stay up late.
At 8 o'clock we watched television
And at 9 o'clock we ate.

The next day Ellie said to me,
'I am going to a new school today.
I better not be late.
My new school is near the bay.'

I rushed home and put my uniform on
And rushed to school.
I met Ellie and she said,
'You're my best friend!' How cool.

Sharlene Gandhi (8)
Raglan Junior School

My Best Friend

My best friend
is who gives
me advice.

My best friend
is who plays with me
and talks to me.

My best friend
is a friend who goes out with me
and makes me laugh.

My best friend
is gentle and kind
but she will just be my friend.

Deeya Dulhumsingh (8)
Raglan Junior School

Spider

I am a little spider
With four legs
On each side.
I spin webs,
Sometimes it breaks
But I will spin anyway.
I trap my food,
Then eat it all.

Dominic Celimon (8)
Raglan Junior School

When Adventure Visits Me

When adventure visits I feel frightened.
When adventure visits I feel brave.

Adventure is here and it feels pretty near
When I'm on my moonlight adventure.

When adventure visits I feel excited.
When adventure visits I feel suspicious
Of spies and *what's that hiding there?*

Was the robbery done in daylight,
In moonlight, in sun or in rain?
I do not know but that spy lives in Spain.

Thanks a lot for the medal and stuff
And your adventure which made me tough!

Lots of adventures racing by,
I'll fall into another through lullaby.

Bye-bye adventure your visit's done,
It's time for me to lie back in the sun.

Shona Burke (7)
Raglan Junior School

Me And My Friends

I have a friend,
She makes me laugh.
I have another friend,
She makes me smile.
I have a very special friend,
She's loving in every way,
She's friendly,
She has hair as brown as chocolate,
Eyes as green as grass.

Andrea Michael (7)
Raglan Junior School

My Own Beach

Love is my hope,
Sometimes I feel hope coming to me.
I feel like I would have my own beach.
I hear peace and quiet.
I feel oceans waving in the sea.
Hope is the only thing I have in this world.

I hear peace and quiet,
It feels like I'm the only one on Earth.
I feel hope and warmth inside me.
I wish sometimes that I had my own beach.
I am very happy,
I wish I could have my own beach.
Hope is love to me,
I feel warm inside my heart.
Love is the only thing I can have in this world,
It will always be there for me,
I have seashells right in my hand
And that is my hope and love!

Shania Sinanan (7)
Raglan Junior School

I'm Happy To Do Everything

I'm happy to be rich.
I'm happy to work.
I'm happy to live.
I'm happy to be alive.
I'm happy to be clever.
I'm happy that I learned things at school.
I'm happy I learned to cook.
I'm happy I learned to do everything!

Jordan Whynn (7)
Raglan Junior School

Music

I love the way the music rocks,
The way it blows me round.

It makes me feel sad and happy.

I love the way the music travels
Each and every day.

I move in music all the time,
It makes me feel lonely,
But when I die the music will take me up,
It will travel with me as long as I go.

Nina McGarvey (8)
Raglan Junior School

Sometimes

Sometimes I feel happy,
Sometimes I feel sad.
Sometimes I feel silly,
Sometimes I feel mad.
Sometimes I feel angry,
Sometimes I feel glad.
Sometimes I feel scared,
Sometimes I feel bad.
Sometimes I feel sleepy,
Sometimes I just feel everything
All at the same time!

George Gaylor (8)
Raglan Junior School

Me And My Family

Me and my cat
We always play.
I try to get her to play
But she always goes and sleeps away.

Me and my brother work together,
When we work together we get the job done.
Me and dog we always run and it's fun,
When he runs I can't catch up.

Me and my dad,
He's sometimes lazy,
He's sometimes supportive,
Very sleepy and I love him a lot.

Me and my mum,
She's very kind, she's very nice,
I love her a lot.

Me and my ball,
My ball always runs,
My ball always jumps,
Balls always bounce.

Canberk Sar (7)
Raglan Junior School

I Wish I Was A Lion

I wish I was a lion eating all the meat.
I wish I was a lion lying in the heat.
I wish I was a lion, king of the beasts.
I wish I was a lion eating all the feasts.
I wish I was a lion laying in the sun.
I wish I was a lion having all the fun.
I wish I was a lion dashing with my paws.
I wish I was a lion that roars, roars, roars.

Amy Godfrey (8)
Raglan Junior School

I Like Going On Holiday

I like going on holiday with my pets.
I like eating ice cream.

My pets are very noisy.
My pets like eating food.

The cats drink milk,
And they chase the dogs around.

Sometimes the cats chase dogs.
The dogs and cats have a sleep in the evening.

They share their baskets.
Sometimes they go too near Grandma.

Lauren Moret (8)
Raglan Junior School

The Jungle

The jungle's the place with giraffes, lions and tigers.
The jungle's the leafiest place.
The jungle's the grassiest place you've ever been.
The jungle's the scariest place in the world.
The jungle has two volcanoes.
The jungle has lots of trees.
The jungle has so many birds.
The jungle has so many tigers.
The jungle has happy animals.

Lucy Fleming (7)
Raglan Junior School

Arsenal

Arsenal are the greatest,
They have the best players in the world
And they aren't afraid to play football!

Arsenal are the greatest,
Bergkamp is the best
And they aren't afraid to play football!

Arsenal are the greatest,
I wonder how many times they've won?
And they aren't afraid to play football!

Josephy Doyle (7)
Raglan Junior School

Monday's Breakfast

Monday's breakfast is very smelly.
Tuesday's breakfast tastes like jelly.
Wednesday's breakfast is very dry.
Thursday's breakfast can fly.
Friday's breakfast is very funny.
Saturday's breakfast is very funky.
But the breakfast I eat on the Sabbath Day
Is the breakfast which is very tasty.

George Platt (8)
Raglan Junior School

A Quiet Poem

It's so quiet that I can hear my pencil scratching.
It's so quiet that I can hear the trees swinging.
It's so quiet that I can hear my mum talking downstairs.
It's so quiet that I can hear my popcorn pop.
It's so quiet that I can hear my dad snoring.
It's so quiet that I can hear the postman whistling.
It's so quiet that I can hear the cars zooming.
It's so quiet that I can hear my door swinging.

Ramin Daswani (8)
Raglan Junior School

Monday's Child

Sunday's child is always funny,
Monday's child is really sunny,
Tuesday's child is extremely cool,
Wednesday's child is very cold,
Thursday's child is very slimy,
Friday's child is really noisy,
But Saturday's child is really sleepy.

Ellie Richards (8)
Raglan Junior School

Sweets

S weets, sweets nothing but sweets!
W hite sweets, orange sweets,
E gg-flavoured sweets, chocolate-flavoured sweets,
E verlasting sweets, chewy sweets,
T alking sweets, shouting sweets,
S weets, sweets, nothing but sweets.

Eve Rosina Gidley (7)
Raglan Junior School

A Quiet Poem

It was so quiet, that I heard a mouse squeak in a hole.
It was so quiet, that I heard my next-door neighbour singing.
It was so quiet, that I heard a girl screaming.
It was so quiet, that I heard a boy playing football.
It was so quiet, that I heard a teacher squeaking her pen.
It was so quiet, that I heard a teacher talking.
It was so quiet, that I heard a cat miaowing.
It was so quiet, that I heard a cup banging.
It was so quiet, that I heard a man shaking.
It was so quiet, that I heard a brush, ha-ha!
It was so quiet, that I heard a boy crying.
It was so quiet, that I heard a girl colouring.

Fateha Ahmed (7)
Raglan Junior School

Monday's Breakfast

Monday's breakfast is always runny,
Tuesday's breakfast is extremely funny,
Wednesday's breakfast is really chilly,
Thursday's breakfast is very silly,
Friday's breakfast is always sweet,
Saturday's breakfast is always a treat;
But the breakfast I have on a Sunday, warms up my feet!

Ayana Charles-Mathurin (8)
Raglan Junior School

My Monster

My monster has huge muscles,
His hair is tangled, knotted and slimy.
My monster's only eyeball is dribbling.
My monster is called *Cyclops!*

Anna Boyes (7)
Raglan Junior School

Football

Football, football is so very fun,
You score goals and people shout,
'We won! We won!'
People say we are the best team in the world
And the other teams go off and blame it on other people.
Football's great,
You should play every day to make you fit
And join in with the game football.

Marianna Savva (7)
Raglan Junior School

My Monster

My monster has a head like a bull,
His chest is big and strong,
His eyes are big like his furry ears,
He is humungous like a mountain,
He makes a dreadful screeching noise,
He gets his big claws and picks you up by the ankles.
I feel shocked because
My monster is the *Minotaur!*

Matthew Bouchacra (8)
Raglan Junior School

My Monster Poem

My monster is very horrible,
He has sharp claws that can go into you.
He has wings,
He has a head like a granny.
My monster is called Harpy,
He has lots and lots of feathers
And a long neck too.

Adnan Aufogul (8)
Raglan Junior School

My Monster

My monster has arms like legs,
His feet are huge,
His head is like a bull's,
He has a massive body,
He makes noises like he is in pain,
He can strangle people,
People are petrified of him,
My monster is the *Minotaur!*

Alexander Georgiou (7)
Raglan Junior School

My Monster

My monster is enormous,
My monster is big and fierce,
He is very strong.
My monster is fast and dangerous,
My monster has massive feet and a gigantic tail.
My monster is *Chimera!*

Joshua Lever (8)
Raglan Junior School

My Monster

My monster has an old robe
And a hunched-up body.
She has snakes for hair,
The snakes are hissing,
My monster is a gorgon!

Songul Uzun (8)
Raglan Junior School

Monday's Breakfast

Monday's breakfast is really funny,
Tuesday's breakfast is always sunny,
Wednesday's breakfast is always silly,
Thursday's breakfast is never chilly,
Friday's breakfast is always light,
Saturday's breakfast is a fright,
But the breakfast that is made on the Sabbath day
Makes you play.

Katie Palmer (8)
Raglan Junior School

My Monster

My monster has hairy arms,
His legs are hairy too.
His head is very hairy,
His body is half man, half bull.
He makes a noise like a hundred elephants.
My monster is the *Minotaur!*

Maria Tryphona (8)
Raglan Junior School

My Monster

My monster has arms like a bear,
He is as dirty as mud,
His head is wild
Black and brown like an old tree,
He has one magic eye,
He hits you with his club.
My monster is *Cyclops!*

Rianna Wray (7)
Raglan Junior School

Monday's Play

Monday's play is really funny,
Tuesday's play is extremely sunny,
Wednesday's play is always silly,
Thursday's play is always chilly,
Friday's play is good for slinging,
Saturday's play is good for pinging
But the play I do on the Sabbath day
Is really such fun!

Elliott Scott (7)
Raglan Junior School

I Wish I Was A Leopard

I wish I was a leopard, jumping through the grass,
I wish I was a leopard, rushing through the path.

I wish I was a leopard, licking all my cubs,
I wish I was a leopard, clawing all the shrubs.

I wish I was a leopard, playing with the boys,
I wish I was a leopard, making all the noise.

Holly Evans (8)
Raglan Junior School

King Of The Swingers

Swing, swing, I can swing through the windy vines.
Swing, swing, I can swing high up in the trees.
It is such fun in the jungle, I would say so myself.
Can you guess what I am?
I'm a gibbon, yes that's me.

Thomas Cocks (7)
Raglan Junior School

The Mouse

Squeak mouse, squeak,
Creak upon the floorboard,
Run into your mouse hole
Run out of your mouse hole.
See a cat.
Screech at the cat,
Drink the cat's milk,
Run out in the wind, *'Eek-eek!'*
Run into your mouse hole.
'Eek-eek!' nice and safe.

Libby Pearce (7)
Raglan Junior School

Colours

The sky is blue, the grass is green,
What other colours on Earth can you see?
The stars are gold, the full moon white,
The black sky shining in the night.
The red-orange sunset brightens up the sky,
All these different colours are pleasing to my eye.
Roses are red, violets are blue,
Colours all around us, for me and you.

Abbie Vivers (7)
Raglan Junior School

My Monster

My monster has a hairy body,
He has got three heads,
He is as big as a tree.
My monster has a slimy snake-like tail.
He makes a very loud roar,
His claw strips through metal.
My monster is *Cerberus!*

Jamie Egan (8)
Raglan Junior School

My Monster

My monster has arms like sharp claws,
His legs are long with pointed claws,
His head has got fuzzy hair,
His body is thin and hairy,
His feathers are on his wings.

His skin is hairy with points sticking out,
His ears are dull and hairy,
His eyes are thin.
My monster is the *Sphinx!*

Trixibel Gurjao (8)
Raglan Junior School

My Monster

My monster has legs,
Two bones stuck together, one bone sticking out.
Her shining, shimmering eyes are like powerful balls.
Her hair is bunched up with slimy, spotted snakes.
Her head is like a witch
And when she looks at someone, they will turn to stone.
The sound she makes is a terrifying croak.
My monster is a *gorgon!*

Shazeea Masud (8)
Raglan Junior School

My Monster

My monster has claws with brown hair,
His feet have hair like a lion's.
His head has horns like a bull's.
His body is as massive as a temple.
I hear terrible roaring in my ears.
He attacks with his horns and
I am paralysed with fear.
My monster is the *Minotaur!*

Remmy Ezeabasili (7)
Raglan Junior School

My Monster

My monster has one eye,
His feet stomp like ten earthquakes,
He has very long hair.
His club has a massive nail,
He's as big as five temples.
He makes big moans all through the day.
He slams his club and I am paralysed with fear.
He is *Cyclops!*

Edward Razzell (8)
Raglan Junior School

My Monster

My monster has huge muscles,
His feet are huge like a club,
His head is like a temple,
My monster has only one eyeball,
His hair is fuzzy, tangled, knotted and slimy.
His body is like a church.
He knows no fear,
My monster is *Cyclops!*

Lois Panayiotou (7)
Raglan Junior School

My Monster

My monster has a body feathery and dirty,
His legs are strong and sturdy.
He is enormous.
My monster makes a noise like thunder.
His actions are fierce,
His claws are sharp and long.
My monster is *Sphinx!*

Chantelle Sheehan (8)
Raglan Junior School

My Monster

My monster has a head like a ball,
Two horns that stick out of his head,
He blows smoke out of his mouth,
His is half man and half bull,
He is enormous,
He is a tall as a high wall,
He is a man-eater,
He grabs people and munches them to broken bones,
I feel really terrified and paralysed with fear.
My monster is called the *Minotaur!*

Peter Whitehead (8)
Raglan Junior School

My Monster

My monster has feathery wings,
Her legs are like claws and very sharp,
She has an ancient woman's head,
Her feathers are as fast as anything,
She has a great body and head,
She has a dreadful scream,
Her claws grab round people's necks.
I am terrified and horrified!
My monster is a *harpy!*

Joshua Cann (7)
Raglan Junior School

My Monster

My monster has large feet
It has massive muscles
On his forehead he has an enormous eye
He has slug's hair
He's got a large body!
He makes horrid noises
He is horrible
My monster is Cyclops.

Thaynara Tocantins (8)
Raglan Junior School

My Monster

My monster has claws the size of a carriage
And eyes of an eagle
The size of a mountain
Fear in its jaws filed with teeth
As wide as a plane
Terror up its sleeves
And stream flying from its nose
My monster is the Sphinx?

Maximillian McKone (8)
Raglan Junior School

My Monster

My monster is uglier than a snake
It has one gigantic eye
Longer hair than a bear
It is greater than the elephants and stronger
Than a great army
My monster's name is Cyclops.

Kyriacos Nahlis (8)
Raglan Junior School

My Monster Poem

My monster has a feathery body like a tree.
It is revolting, huge like a slimy mountain.
My monster is a fierce monster.
Her head is uglier than a tree.
It has wings and the wings are crinkly.
Even the rings are shiny and gold.
Her voice is a screeching noise.
My monster is the Sphinx.

Benedine Antwi (7)
Raglan Junior School

My Monster Poem

My monster has massive arms covered with feathers
Its claws are very sharp, very white
Her head is like a young woman
My monster's body looks like an enormous wicked crow
She is as enormous as a temple
She screeched and went red in the face
My monster is a siren!

Millie Rickleton (7)
Raglan Junior School

My Monster

My monster has frightening arms
Long hair and just one eye
He has horrifying feet, claws like a dinosaur's
It is as enormous as a temple
Hideous and ugly, roaring in horror
Hits them round the head with a bat
He roars and roars and roars.

Sean Kelly (7)
Raglan Junior School

My Monster Poem

My monster has hairy arms.
Its feet are claws with pencils on top.
He has beady eyes like he is staring at me.
He can blow you to Greece in a day.
It is dreadful, it roars!
He will give you a headache.
You can turn into stone!
My monster is Cerberus.

Tommy Little (7)
Raglan Junior School

My Monster Poem

My monster's head has an eye as red as fire.
His feet are as green as grass.
He is stinky and cold.
He is as big as Ancient Greece.
Its hair goes right down his back
He makes me run from his ugly and revolting sight.
He lives in Greece.
My monster is the Cyclops!

Harriet Brown (7)
Raglan Junior School

My Monster

My monster has hair arms and sharp claws.
His legs are ugly and fat,
His head is like a hairy, fuzzy thing,
He has a gigantic body as huge as a temple,
He makes a dreadful roar,
If he gets mad, he will eat ten people for his meal.
I feel scared and frightened.
My monster is the *Sphinx!*

Emily Coelho (7)
Raglan Junior School

My Monster

My monster's arms are as big as a giant's.
Her legs are as small as a mouse.
Her head is an ancient woman's,
Her eyes are as yellow as moonlight.
Her feathers are like dead leaves,
She is as big as the Mediterranean Sea.
She makes croaking noises that can blow a house down.
She grabs your leg and squeezes so hard
You could pass out.
I am frightened and I shake in fear.
My monster is a Harpy!

Michelle Eghan (8)
Raglan Junior School

My Monster

My monster has a head like a witch
It has hair like snakes
The body is as shiny as a ring
The nose is as long as a thumb.

He makes sounds like a sword slashing
He runs up behind you
Picks you up and chucks you down
I paralyse you with fear
My monster is a Gorgon!

Heidi Welch (8)
Raglan Junior School

When Stephanie Say

When Stephanie say wink
yuh better blink

When Stephanie say tall
yuh better shrink

When Stephanie say stand
yuh better fall

When Stephanie say silent
yuh better call

When Stephanie say forget
yuh better remember

When Stephanie say April
yuh better September

When Stephanie say patterned
yuh better plain

When Stephanie say wind
yuh better rain.

Stephanie Stevens (8)
Raglan Junior School

My Monster

My monster has fiery wings and sharp claws
Feet as gigantic as a mansion
Frizzy hair with maggots in it
My monster makes a screech
A dreadful noise
She grabs you by the neck
And is as spooky as most
My monster is a Harpy.

Ben Salvi (7)
Raglan Junior School

When Jake Say

When Jake say easy
yuh better tough

When Jake say smooth
yuh better rough

When Jake say postpone
yuh better game

When Jake say nobody
yuh better fame

When Jake say truth
yuh better lie

When Jake say live
yuh better die.

Jake Smith (8)
Raglan Junior School

My Monster

My monster has sharp, shiny claws
It has hairy and curly fur
She has furry, fluffy wings
Her eyes are very scary and as red as fire
She's got a spiky, furry tail
She is very strong and fears nothing
She is very scary everywhere
Her tail is burnt at the tip of it
My monster is a Sphinx!

Sophia Evangelides (8)
Raglan Junior School

When Chloe Say

When Chloe say swim
yuh better drown

When Chloe say jeans
yuh better gown

When Chloe say glitter
yuh better yukky

When Chloe say clean
yuh better mucky.

Chloé Green (8)
Raglan Junior School

What I Love About You

I love the way you look at me,
Your eyes so bright and blue.
I love the way you kiss me,
Your lips so soft and smooth.

I love the way you make me so happy,
And the ways you show you care.
I love the way you say, 'I love you,'
And the way you're always there.

I love the way you touch me,
Always sending chills down my spine.
I love that you are with me
And glad that you are mine.

Roshni Adatia (10)
Reddiford School

The Ant And The Dove

A black, petite ant strolled along the bank of the flowing stream
The hot, golden sun burnt his back
Tired and thirsty he walked slowly towards the stream.
The tiny ant fell into the sparkling water
and was carried away by the rushing stream.

A white, beautiful dove sitting on an emerald, tall tree
Spotted the minute ant floating
She plucked a leaf with veins from the tree
And threw it into the blowing stream.
The ant grabbed onto the green leaf and floated safely
And cried, 'Thank you! I'll help you some day!'

Days later, a mean and sly birdcatcher came under the massive tree
To set a trap for the kind dove
By putting brown lime twigs under the massive tree
The ebony ant seeing the tricky birdcatcher trying to catch his friend
Became worried and frightened
And suddenly thought of a plan of what he was going to do.

The diminutive ant crept up and stung the horrible bird catcher.
Screaming loudly in pain the birdcatcher hopped on one foot.
Hearing the noise the petrified dove quickly flew away
The brave ant smiled to himself, *one good turn deserves another.*

Afzal Roked (9)
Reddiford School

What Am I?

I travel at night
I have very good hearing
I can see in the dark
I swoop and search for mice to eat
I am very wise
I have a beak which is like a tip of a Concorde.

Thairshan Suthakaran (10)
Reddiford School

Elves And Carpenters

When darkness falls like a bird
noon utters a word,
I creep around the streets
with bare, stockinged feet
and patter through the night,
looking for the sight
of a cobbler's house

It was tucked in an alley
that was cold, dark and shabby.
So I peeped in and saw,
through the cobbler's door
one piece of material to sew
I blew on my hands and got ready to go.

He was now prosperous,
but had not forgotten us.
They hid behind curtains,
watched us so certain
next day we returned
but soon we had learned,
how clothes felt so soft
with a continuous waft
of clean soap.

This was no time to mope
we dragged off our rags
and danced hand in hand
our elfin ears jumping
hearts loud and thumping
happy as could be
to make a carpenter glee.

Nilam Ark (10)
Reddiford School

Little Red Riding Wolf

Little Red Riding Wolf as sweet as can be
Skipped off to see his grandma for tea
But in the deepest, darkest corner of the wood
The Big Bad Girl patiently stood.

The Big Bad Girl loved little wolves like him
Because she could consume them with one big grin
Now the Big Bad Girl was as hungry as a bear
And she desperately wanted her share

The Big Bad Girl knew Little Red Riding Wolf was going to see his gran
She decided to quickly make her plan
The Big Bad Girl soon knew what she was going to do
She was going to eat Little Red Riding Wolf's gran and have him too

She went to Grandma's house but when she got there
Amazingly enough no one was here
The Big Bad Girl went upstairs
And sat on one of the comfortable chairs

Soon Little Red Riding Wolf arrived
The Big Bad Girl was quite surprised
'Gosh that was jolly quick,'
She pretended to be very sick

Little Red Riding Wolf came in
Carrying a great, big biscuit tin
'Ah! Grandma you don't look well today!'
'Well actually I'm feeling okay.'

In strode the real gran
The Big Bad Girl just flicked on the fan
As if she didn't care.

Far from afraid, Grandma Wolf was irate
The Big Bad Girl was soon chased out of the gate!

Jeevan Dhillon (9)
Reddiford School

Cinderella

Poor Cinderella treated like a slave
Very hardworking and she is quite brave
She just scrubs and doesn't make a sound
The handsome prince invited them all
To his wonderful birthday ball
The ugly sisters dressed up fine
But Cinderella had to go to bed at nine
The sisters went out in fancy dress
While Cinderella was left with the mess
In a flash of light the fairy godmother came
And waved her wand and called her name
'Cinderella, you shall go to the ball
Now you are the fairest of them all.'
She wore a beautiful sparkling dress
She looked better than all the rest
In a golden coach she went
Smelling of expensive scent
She danced with the prince all night
He loved her at first sight
The clock struck 12 midnight
Cinderella had a big fright
Her beautiful clothes were all gone
Her rags appeared, she was in tears
The next morning the prince came
To claim whose it was
He tried everyone but then, the last one,
Cinderella!
It fitted like a wink
From that day on they had days that were like gold
And that was how the story was told.

Aliysha Modi (10)
Reddiford School

Wild Animals

As I explored the African savannah,
The overgrown plants and trees hung over my head,
The soil beneath my feet was scattered here and there,
I tiptoed my way through the tall brown grass
making sure no one could hear me,
It was like a desert to me.

I could hear the fierce roars of the wild lions tearing flesh brutally,
The king of the savannah full of pride,
Feasting on the best meat,
The lionesses preened their baby cubs whilst lying on the ground,
The lion family are dangerous wild animals,

The cheetahs were sprinting madly waiting to pounce on their prey,
Swift impalas dashed as fast as they could,
But were soon caught by some fiercesome cheetahs,
They raced around everywhere
Marking their territory wherever they went,
The cheetahs are the fastest wild animals.

As night came the leopards growled in the distance,
Their sly looking eyes gleamed in the darkness,
Their spotty coat shone in the darkness,
They strolled elegantly with strength and agility,
These leopards are the cunning predators.

The wind brushed against my face as I tiptoed,
The leaves were as crispy as a crisp packet,
The hairs on the back of my neck went up as I shivered,
I kept a look out in case anyone was there,
The plains were beautiful but daunting.

Sheethal Jethwa (8)
Reddiford School

Autumn

As I walk through my magnificent garden,
The bright, morning sun shines in my eyes.
Floating dandelions fall calmly onto the crispy leaves,
Which have changed their colour from emerald-green,
To a beautiful, fiery gold.

Soon the sweet aroma of honey beckons me,
But I will not be tempted anymore.
A small nest has fallen to the ground,
So I look inside and I see a cute robin,
Resting as gracefully as a swan.

Squirrels are nibbling on the scarlet berries,
Then a sweet bramble breeze refreshes me and
It sounds like a ghost moving swiftly
I can also hear a faint sound,
Of a calm dove cooing.

Hedgehogs are scuttling around,
Trying to find their burrows frantically.
All the animals are hibernating now,
And the falling leaves have been scattered.
Do you know what I'm trying to say?

Anjali Roopram (8)
Reddiford School

Kangaroos

K angaroos are soft and cuddly,
A nd they bounce like basketballs,
N ow there are 50 kinds of kangaroos in Australia,
G rasses so eager to be eaten by them,
R acing outside the red outback of Australia,
O utwardly confident in listening for dangerous enemies,
O utstandingly beady eyes,
S trong back legs are well used for jumping.

Leya Peshavaria (8)
Reddiford School

Dragons

You might have seen them in your dreams
You might have even met one.
But one night they woke me up,
Boy was I surprised!

Thousands of them, flying around,
Like bumblebees.
One actually saw me, I got frightened,
Would it kill me?

I would just have to wait and see,
As it came towards me.
But what was this?
He picked me up and put me on his back.

I think it's a lift off!
Up, up and away!
Where do we go?
To a distant land?
Well I guess you'll never know!

Aakesh Patel (8)
Reddiford School

Who's Who?

They are grey or brown,
They never have a frown,
Everyone loves them,
They're so gentle and sweet,
But they absolutely love to eat.

They have sharp teeth and paws
And fearsome claws,
With long, furry tails
And can sniff out mysterious trails.

Do you know the answer?

Ayomikun Obileye (8)
Reddiford School

Tiger Tiger

Walking and striding,
very regal and proud,
man's oldest foe,
his snarl is so loud.

Strong and bold,
on its majestic stride,
old tales have told,
from this beast you will hide.

Biggest cat of all,
stalking for an ambush,
every prey it will maul
hiding in the bush.

My favourite feline,
the tiger from the Far East,
a creature so divine,
truly a beautiful beast.

Keval Mehta (9)
Reddiford School

All About Animals And Insects

Fat animals, slim animals
Insects that can fly
Cuddly animals, furry animals
Animals that can die.

Animals can be big
Insects are small
Animals can be kings of the world
And so can the insects that are tall.

Animals like watching TV
Insects get filmed for DVD
Animals like listening under the sea
While they drink tea.

Anjani Saujani (9)
Reddiford School

The Gingerbread Man

There once lived an old man,
Living with him was an old woman,
One day she was making a tasty gingerbread man,
She heard a sound and the oven door flung open and out came Gingy.

Before you could say stop, Gingy was gone,
Down the road he met a cow,
Who scarcely saw him,
But the old man's treat wouldn't stop running,

Turning off into the next road Gingy met a horse,
Horsy saw a nice snack, it was Gingy,
Horse tried to catch him,
But Gingy was too fast.

Gingy ran on and came to a river, he didn't know now how to swim,
Suddenly Gingy saw a fox,
The fox grinned and said, 'Hops onto my tail
And I will take you across.'
So Gingy hopped onto fox's tail.

'Hop onto my back or you will sink,' cried fox.
Gingy knew what would happen and phoned Miss Riding Hood,
'Can you help me, I am with a fox and in deep trouble.'
'I will be there,' she replied.

'Actually hop on my nose,' said Foxy.
When they got to the other side Foxy threw Gingy into the air,
When suddenly Miss Riding Hood caught Gingy in a net
                                        and shot Foxy,
Now she has a fox skin coat and a bite to eat.

Jaimien Dave (9)
Reddiford School

Cinderella

Cinderella working morning till night,
She lit fires, carried water, cooked and washed.
She worked till she was weary,
But had no bed to go to.

She slept by the hearth in the cinders
So she always appeared dirty and dusty
And this is why her ugly stepsisters
Named her Cinderella.

The ugly stepsisters mocked and ridiculed her
All day long, but poor Cinderella wept
And cried silent tears
Sitting by her dear mother's grave.

An invitation arrived from the King's palace
Inviting all young women to attend a festival
For the king was in search of a bride for his son.

The delighted ugly stepsisters
Immediately sent for Cinderella to tend to their needs.
Cinderella begged to go but stood no chance.

Cinderella wept and in a flash appeared
Her fairy godmother granting her every wish.
With a wave of her magic wand she turned
Her old rags into a stunning gold gown.

Cinderella arrived in style in a majestic golden carriage
All eyes upon her. She was soon approached by the Prince
His eyes not letting her out of his sight
And they danced to the music till midnight.

Serena Mehta (9)
Reddiford School

The Three Fat Pigs

Once there were three pigs
Who decided to act big
Off they went into the big wide world
And kept their word
To build homes of their own
Without a moan
Number one was of straw
Built with his own pawy-paw-paw
Number two decided on sticks
Built with many exciting tricks
Number three thought of bricks
He wasn't thick.
Along came Mr Wolf
Looking for some raw
'Little pig, little pig, let me in.'
Said little pig, 'Jump in the bin.'
Huff, huff.
Pig was as dead as a lump of lead.
Next was number two,
'Little pig, little pig, let me through.'
'Oh,' said pig, 'no way!'
Huff, huff and pig passed away.
Number three with the brains
Had made a class plan including a drain
Said, 'Welcome Mr Wolf, you have come for your raw?'
'Yes,' said Mr Wolf with a sign with his paw.
'Oh no,' said number three, 'watch the drain!'
As Mr Wolf writhed in pain.

Mithulan Thavatheva (9)
Reddiford School

The Gingerbread Man

Once there lived a smart man with his adoring wife
Who above most wanted a gingerbread child
The wife baked a man who suddenly came to life

He cried, 'Jog jog as fast as you can,
You can't catch me the gingerbread man,'
The man and his wife sprinted as fast as they could
But they still could not catch the speedy gingerbread man.

On his way the gingerbread man met a cow
And challenged the cow to catch him
'Moo moo,' cried the cow as he plodded after the gingerbread man
'I didn't know that Gingerbread Man could run so fast,'
Mooed the dopey cow

Then the gingerbread man met a handsome horse
Who used all his force to catch the arrogant gingerbread man
But still he could not capture the bragging gingerbread man

Then poor gingerbread man came to a vast river
Which smelt of disgusting liver
'We've got him now,' bellowed the crowd

Then all of a sudden a sly fox appeared to see all the commotion
The gathered crowd all feared, and fell silent
As the sly fox licked his lips

'Hey, Ginger man I'll take you across the river on my back,'
Hissed the cunning fox,
So the gingerbread man jumped on the fox's back and galloped away
The wily fox yelled, 'There's a branch ahead, jump onto my toes.'

The gingerbread man jumped onto the devious fox's toe
Then the shrewd fox shrieked, 'You'll sink down there,
Hop onto my nose,'
So the gingerbread man leapt to the fox's nose

Within a blink of an eye
The scheming fox tossed his head and flung the gingerbread man
Into his wide gaping mouth.

Amish Mehta (9)
Reddiford School

Goldilocks And The Three Bears

Deep in the forest lived three bears,
Daddy bear, Mummy bear and baby bear.
One sunny morning, while the porridge was piping hot,
The three bears decided to go for a walk.

Goldilocks came skipping through the forest,
And spotted the three bears' lovely, little cottage.
She sniffed her way to the delicious porridge,
And found three bowls on the table.

The porridge in the first bowl was too hot,
And the porridge in the second bowl was way too cold,
But the porridge in third bowl was perfect.
So she ate all the porridge in the bowl
And wiped her mouth with a serviette.

Then she saw three chairs,
The first one was extremely rare,
And the second one had a picture of a bear,
But the third chair was neutrally consumed.
Though when she sat on the chair it broke into diminutive pieces.

She made her way upstairs,
And strolled into the bedroom of the three bears.
The first bed was truly hard,
And the second bed was way too soft
But the third bed was exceptionally cosy.

She tucked herself into this comfortable bed and fell fast asleep.
Soon the three bears arrived and what did they see on the table,
Three bowls with one empty bowl and a chair nearby
                              that was disabled.
Then they heard some snoring coming from upstairs,
And wondered what Goldilocks was doing on baby bear's bed
When Goldilocks woke up she was afraid of these three bears,
And she never went into the forest again.

Trushna Patel (10)
Reddiford School

The Hare And The Tortoise

One fine sunny day
The hare was heard to say,
'I can beat anyone in a race!
With my speedy and blistering pace.'
The tortoise slowly walked up to the hare
All of the animals stopped to stare.
The tortoise said, 'Then why don't you race me?'
The hare replied, 'I can beat you hopping on one knee.'
So next day, at the clearing,
All of the animals were laughing and jeering
And saying the hare was surely going to win.
Having listened to this, the tortoise wore a huge, sly grin.
With a shot of a gun the race started
The hare and the tortoise had already parted.
The steady tortoise plodded along
The hare was relaxed and hummed a song.
The hare sat down as he was far ahead
Then decided to take a nap instead.
The tortoise carefully came walking by
And then heaved a great sigh.
As the tortoise touched the finish line
The hare felt a shiver down his arrogant spine.

Rushil Malde (10)
Reddiford School

The Gingerbread Man

Granny was making a gingerbread man
Oh! he looked like he was getting a tan
A faint voice shouted, 'Let me out'
Granny opened the oven door thinking nowt
Out he escaped and sprinted across the floor
Wanted to get in the open so threw himself out the door

He ran through the meadows
Following his own shadow
Met a horse and cow
Having a little row
There he came to a nasty river
Thought he was going to slither
Then he met a friendly fox
Who said, 'I'll take you over to the locks.

Jump on my tail,
Wait, I'm turning pale
Jump on my back
Oh! I think my bone is going to crack!
You're still too heavy, jump on my nose
That feels strange, don't tickle me with your toes

I'm paddling as fast as I can go
Hey, can you help me by using your arms to row?'
The fox gave a sniggering sound
Then tossed him in the air round and round
Down came the gingerbread man sailing fast
Straight into the fox's mouth at last
That was the end of him
If only he knew how to swim
This just wasn't fair
But, life is full of things you just can't bear!

Ahsan Jamil (9)
Reddiford School

Cinderella

Poor Cinderella treated like a slave
But she was always very brave
As she wept
And nearly slept
On the cold floor
That she felt no more,
The little girl scolded and yelled at
For her not to sleep on a tiny mat
When she didn't get any money
She didn't win any honey.

As a messenger came to the castle
He delivered a parcel
When the sisters had approached the letter
Cinderella tried to do better
There the fairy godmother appeared
When Cinderella's tears had disappeared
A golden carriage made for the princess
And changed Cinderella's dress
Happily Cinderella skipped in
On she went with no little tin.

When Cinderella arrived at the palace
She had no idea where to go
As the sisters were shocked to see her
The prince fell in love with her instantly
They danced and it struck twelve
'I have to go,' Cinderella said quickly
She rushed and was dressed back into rags

There came a messenger who asked,
'Does this belong to anyone,' he asked royally
'This is my slipper,' admitted Cinderella
She tried the slipper and it fitted her
And her and the prince were married
And lived happily ever after.

Mamtaa Patel (9)
Reddiford School

The Gingerbread Man

The old lady heard a little voice
'Let me out! Let me out!' the little voice cried.
She opened the oven
And out it leapt.
'My gingerbread man!' the old lady wept.
Across it dashed along the floor
And right out of the kitchen door.
The little man ran as fast as he could,
The pig and the cow ran as fast as they would,
And the old lady shouted, 'Come back! Come back!'
But the little man just wouldn't return.
He skipped along merrily,
Singing away his merry song,
'Run, run as fast as you can!'
'You can't catch me, I'm the gingerbread man.'
Though, singing away his merry tune
He came to a river very soon.
He stopped, he gasped, and he said, 'I'll die.'
But then saw Foxy with his eye.
Now Foxy just began to feel
That he would like a gingerbread meal.
He put Ginger on his back
And took him to the river bank.
Ah, cunning Foxy had a plan,
That poor Ginger couldn't scan.
He tossed him up in the air,
And ate the bread in one big bite,
Foxy didn't leave a crumb to spare,
But said, 'Oh lovely, yum, yum in my tum!'

Serena Patel (10)
Reddiford School

On Eagle Wings

How I would like to fly
With the eagles soaring high.
Is it not a lot of dreams
To fly free on eagle wings?

Why birds are the most magnificent things
But above all I adore the eagle.
How they fly on their feathered wings.
I have never met a person
Who does not share my love of eagles.

The way they hunt is quite amazing.
I hope this poem brings to you
The love of eagles I have
Through my entire body.

Alexander Price (9)
Reddiford School

Foxy Loxy

There lived a chick called Chicken Licken
He thought the sky was falling
So he went to tell the king
On his way he met his friends
Henny Penny, Cocky Locky, Drakey Lakey,
Ducky Lucky, Gander Lander and Turkey Lurkey.
As they were walking a fox jumped out
His name was Foxy Loxy
He licked his lips round and round
As though they all looked tasty
Foxy Loxy lied to them
And instead he took them to his den
In one second they were eaten up
They were finished . . .

Jasminder Sagoo (10)
Reddiford School

Sunflowers

Sunflowers reaching to the sky,
Like a beautiful butterfly.
Sunflowers growing tall and high,
Past the bushes and the flies.

Sunflower oh! Sunflower,
How beautiful you are,
With your golden petals
And your stem of strength.

Sunflower oh! Sunflower,
You always brighten my day.
So please promise me,
That you won't go away.

Arjun Puri (9)
Reddiford School

Winter's Feast

Taste a spoon of flower petals,
Eat a plate of snow,
Sip a glass of rain.

Red of a rose,
Orange of a fiery marigold,
Yellow of a sunflower,
Green of the leaves,
Blue of the sea,
Indigo cat-faced pansies
Violet iris frill.

Make a pizza of ice,
Eat a bowl of ice cream clouds
Before you start your work.

Cindy Asokan (8)
Reddiford School

Captured By The Pirates

I filled my tummy with goody, goody snacks,
Watching TV, I felt a bit drowsy and thirsty,
Reached out to get a glass of water, but couldn't

On a deck of a ship stood I, my hands tied back on a pole.
With bulging eyes with red, thick beard,
Like Captain Hook in the Peter Pan movie,
Limping, a man appeared.
Shivered I, like a mouse in a trap.

The man came closer grinding his rotten teeth,
I tried to get my hands free, but it was no use,
But I thought of a great idea,
I turned around and pulled the rope with hope
And quickly slipped through the cutting rope.

'Stop him,' said the Captain
I was surrounded by the most ugly pirates
'Help me, help me,' I started crying.
'Wake up, it is only a dream,' said my mum smiling.

Venkatesh Surendran (8)
Reddiford School

The Ode To Uluru (Ayres Rock)

While travelling through the outback I met
A kind Aborigine just and wise
Who cried, 'My ancestors from Anangu
Are all dead. Their tribe will live on with me,
Though. Their cadavers lie here with us now
Rotting away with the sand whilst we live.'
When I look down at the sacred red soil,
I see the blood from those who are wounded
Wounded from the pains of others deaths here.
The digging of nails into their hearts,
To remind them of the heartbreaking pain
That they suffered, and still suffer now here.
I see it in the eyes of the people.

Lauren Brett (10)
St Nicholas CE Primary School, Shepperton

A Monument To Stone Age Man

On top of a hill on Salisbury Plain,
a monument to Stone Age man.
A circle of colossal grey stones,
megaliths from a time long ago.
Some standing, some fallen, some resting aloft,
silent, mysterious, their secrets untold.
No message, no words to tell us the story,
of the meaning of a monument to Stone Age man.
For 3,000 years they have stood,
never changing, never moving,
only watching history unfold.
When we have inhabited Mars,
will we have discovered the secrets,
of a monument to Stone Age man?

Elise Matthews (10)
St Nicholas CE Primary School, Shepperton

Millennium Dome

It looks like the sun on a cold day,
covered in white snow,
surrounded by the rest of London.
What a spectacular show.

The visitors walk in and out,
at the London Dome,
then they get into their cars,
and start their travel home.

The roads are slippery
with layers of ice
the trees are glistening
all looking very nice

What a wonderful day at the London Dome,
with the weather so bad, it's good to be home.

Becky Percival (11)
St Nicholas CE Primary School, Shepperton

The Eiffel Tower That Stole My Pink Shoe

I met a strange man,
Sitting by the sea,
In a dark blue coat,
Now who could he be?
He stared in my eyes,
And then he told me,
'Listen to my words,
My little pretty;
The Eiffel Tower,
A beautiful thing,
As tall as the sky,
Makes you want to sing,
The Eiffel Tower,
As French as can be,
The language is hard,
But as you can see,
Nothing is hard, if -
You see what I mean.'
I stared at his face,
He stared at mine too,
He knelt in the sand,
And stole my pink shoe,
'You'll never be good,
At French just like me!'
Then he stood upright,
And got up to flee,
Next shouted back,
'You'll never catch me.'

Rosanna Parsonage (11)
St Nicholas CE Primary School, Shepperton

King Knossos

In all the hustle bustle stands an old weary thing;
tourists looking never to really know the secrets haunting there,
and in my mind I see them now, what a grand place to live.
The heat that crept up this place and their distraught time;
memories lost and missing, waiting until the empire is found,
the Minoans gone, king and all but what is left tells us
that although they lived so long ago their mysterious ways
                                              were often wiser.
Yet all the tales and legends of labyrinth and Minotaur
were all but nonsense.
The real truth is at the heart; knowledge and strength
on an island called Crete, a great palace stands tall
passionately carved into time!

Mark Forrest (11)
St Nicholas CE Primary School, Shepperton

Disguised As A Poem

Many worlds live within its icy façade
Layer upon layer, standing so tall,
Reflecting each other's magnificence,
And the madness of the city it belongs.

So many worlds have heard of its existence,
Many came from near and far, to witness
A world in the heavens, and to touch the
Shroud of billowy clouds that surrounds it.

Its outline which once played on the landscape,
Plays no more, stands no more, it is but dust,
Leaving a legacy of fear and terror
In a world where we can no longer trust.

Heidi Jagger (11)
St Nicholas CE Primary School, Shepperton

The Millennium Dome

There once was a man who went on a trip
To the bubble-like Millennium Dome,
He said, it's as tall as a sailing ship,
As deep and mysterious as a wood,
Round as an igloo, ice up to its tip.
'But no, please wait!' the dome called out to him,
The echoing voice going round in his head;
'There's much, much more to me than what you see,
For I was born in 1999,
And before I could catch my breath,
I slowly died in 2001.
Yet cannot you see a glimmer still exists,
Nothing inside me . . . not yet anyway,
Just empty inside   no one to love me,
It feels like I'm rotting away . . .
My short days of glory, been and gone.'

Helena Sugden (11)
St Nicholas CE Primary School, Shepperton

Eiffel Tower

As I was gazing out on the sea one day
I saw, a towering building leap up
Into the sky . . . around it they lay,
Tourists, from everywhere around the world,
And faces cold, during the month of May
The building all grey looked down on everyone
All around the rusty top could be seen,
The base that stopped them, from saying I won,
And from the sky thunder likes to shout out,
'This is the Eiffel Tower, come and look,
All eyes will look, up at me, with no doubt!'

Lauren Thorpe (10)
St Nicholas CE Primary School, Shepperton

Thingamajigs

I just saw the thingamajigs walking down our street a . . . a . . .
Oh what's its name?
I'll try to count to three.

I ate a thingamabob and I swallowed it down like a . . . a . . .
Oh what's its name?
I'll try and find out in a dictionary.

I just saw a what do you call it . . . a . . . a . . .
Oh what's its name?
I'll see if I am thirteen.

Those thingamajigs just kiss my sister, yuk! They were like a . . . a . . .
Oh what's its name?
I'll run away just in case they kiss me.

I just saw a thingamabob on our rooftop . . . a . . . a . . .
Oh what's its name?
I'll look on the TV box.

I just kicked a what do you call it . . . a . . . a . . .
Oh what's its name?
I'll play on my tambourines.

Those thingamabobs are like a thingamajig a . . .
What do you call it, a . . . a . . .
Oh what's its name?
I don't know.

Yueh Chang (9)
St Nicholas CE Primary School, Shepperton

The Tower Of Fame

The Leaning Tower Of Pisa still stands
With posture and grace; wise, has memories,
Famous from Europe to the distant lands
Which are uncovered, undiscovered, yes,
The tower of fame, I'll call that its name,
'One day the tower might fall!' one might guess,
But let's think our tower will win the game . . .

Emerald Lewis (11)
St Nicholas CE Primary School, Shepperton

Hampton Court

It's stood there for ages, with a horrible stare,
The king that mocked them and the coldest gusts of wind,
That makes you feel so cold, right down to the bare bone.
The *woos* of the ghosts make you want to turn around,
And the clunks of feet on the hard stone staircases.
The wails of ghosts, and screaming Catherine Howard,
It's a haunted place, don't even try to approach.
Of course, I'm talking about Hampton Court Palace.
An evil, horrible place and very spooky.
Even now, 2004 this year, right now,
Will we ever know the secrets of Hampton Court?

Alice Rush (10)
St Nicholas CE Primary School, Shepperton

Sweets

S ugared sherbet sings on the seashore
W hizzing Winders wait for William
E nergetic eclairs excitedly eat everything
E xcellent Echos emerging from England
T ired Tic Tacs talking together
S illy Softmints stupidly swim swiftly.

Holly Candlin (9)
St Nicholas CE Primary School, Shepperton

What Am I?

I am big and fat
I live in a farm
I lay around
I have four legs
I am always dirty
Because I roll around in mud
I eat corn and mostly anything
What am I?

Bradley Kelsall (9)
St Nicholas CE Primary School, Shepperton

Chocolate

At 3.15 I get out of school,
And I need something really cool.
Mmm chocolate.

I love chocolate the best of all,
Peppermint, toffee, big or small.
Mmm chocolate.

I'll eat chocolate in all shapes or sizes,
Eggs, beans in every disguise.
Mmm chocolate.

Christmas and Easter are the best,
Give me the chocolate never mind the rest
Mmm chocolate.

Hannah Reichel (9)
St Nicholas CE Primary School, Shepperton

Football

Football is fun
it makes you run,
it's a big sport
it has lots of support,
he scored a goal
it was Ashley Cole,
tackle straight
or you will be late,
he got a red card
it was
Steven Gerrard.

Ben Williamson (9)
St Nicholas CE Primary School, Shepperton

Planes

Planes fly through the whistling wind.
Over the beautiful sunset.
Through bubbly clouds.
I look out the window
And see the amazing, rushing wind.
The sun sets
Everyone sleeps.
It's quiet,
But I'm still awake
Watching the moon.
It looks like . . .
Cream cheese . . .
So . . .
Calm . . .
And . . .

Rhys Sweetland (10)
St Nicholas CE Primary School, Shepperton

Spring Is . . .

S pring is the time when you get lovely flowers.
P oppies come out to say hello.
R abbits and sheep have their young.
I can't wait till butterflies come.
N ewborn lambs come out to play.
G oing to be summer soon, hooray!

Georgia Fuller (9)
St Nicholas CE Primary School, Shepperton

Clouds

Clouds clouds
In the sky
Clouds clouds
Floating by.

Clouds clouds
Moving fast
Clouds clouds
Rushing past.

Clouds clouds
Over me
Making shapes
What can they be?

Racing cars
That push and pull
Witches faces
Cotton wool.

Clouds clouds
In the sky
Clouds clouds
Floating by.

Dale Wallace (10)
St Nicholas CE Primary School, Shepperton

Chocolate

Chocolate is yummy
It fills my tummy
Chocolate is best
But it makes a mess
It's on the floor
It's on the door
Who'll clear it up?
Not me!

Dillon Neagle (9)
St Nicholas CE Primary School, Shepperton

Falling Down The Stairs

Walk s
   l
   o
   w
  5 to g
      o
    Trip! B
        a
        n
        g!
    Ouch! W
           h
           a
           c
           k!
      Help! A
              w
              w!
        Whaa! S
                p
                l
                a
                t!
                Daddy.

Robert Stevenson (10)
St Nicholas CE Primary School, Shepperton

What Am I?

W hen you run it runs faster than you
A lot of it could get you wet
T he glass has it in, but you have not.
E asy to get in this country, but not in some
R ough, I don't think so.

I t just flows and flows,
S wiftly down through the lock.

Harry Martin (9)
St Nicholas CE Primary School, Shepperton

My Little Sister Evie

My little sister Evie
Cries all night,
What shall I do
When she's out of sight?

My little sister Evie
I sing her lovely lullabies,
What shall I do
If she's pretending to close her eyes.

My little sister Evie
Makes me so proud,
But what shall I do
When she's crying out loud?

Amy Cook (9)
St Nicholas CE Primary School, Shepperton

An Acrostic About A Limerick Poem

L imericks are nonsense
I n time might make sense
M aybe they're unusual.
E ternity will know,
R edeemed by time alone.
I mpossible to understand first time
C ause disorder in the mind
K iller of logic and sense
S ense will prevail in time.

Shaun McGuinness (9)
St Nicholas CE Primary School, Shepperton

Exams

Why do we have them?
Everyone hates them!
Heart beats
Knees shake
It feels like we're on
An earthquake.

People get worried
What if they fail?
Hearts beat
Knees shake
It feels like we're on
An earthquake.

Georgia Anthony (10)
St Nicholas CE Primary School, Shepperton

Tabby Cats

T abbies, tabbies, tabbies, I love tabbies
A bout and out
B aby birds in their nests
B ored cats climb trees
Y ou better watch out

C ats creep curiously
A fter angry animals
T o tops of trees
S uddenly . . .

Holly Jackson (10)
St Nicholas CE Primary School, Shepperton

Not Now Natalie

Not now Natalie
It's only half-past eight,
Go back to bed
They haven't opened the gate.

Not now Natalie
You have to go to school,
You're going to be late
I'll meet you in the hall.

Not now Natalie
We're not in the mood,
If you play with us
We'll get you some food.

Not now Natalie
Sarah just fell,
It's nearly time to go
There goes the bell.

Not now Natalie
You're five minutes late,
Go and have supper
They nearly shut the gate.

Not now Natalie
You're bedtime has gone,
Go straight to bed
Put your PJs on.

Tasnima Bashir (9)
St Nicholas CE Primary School, Shepperton

What Am I?

I like to run
I think it's fun
I'm round and plump
I like the dump
I have padded feet
I love my treats
I chew on hats
Plus mats
I jump on tables
I grind up cables.

What am I?

Bethany Conyers (9)
St Nicholas CE Primary School, Shepperton

What Am I?

I have four rubber paws,
Razor-sharp claws.

I have a very wet nose,
And I don't wear clothes.

I have very fluffy ears,
I don't have any fears.

I leave paw prints on the tables,
I sometimes chew cables.

   What am I?

Olivia Haywood (9)
St Nicholas CE Primary School, Shepperton

My Dolphin

We bought her off the Internet
A funny way to buy a pet

She lives in the Scottish sea
Miles away from me

Lives in a pod of seven
Must be her idea of Heaven

Glides along with grace
She really likes to race

Her coat is silvery-blue
There is nothing else she can't do

She leaps in and out of the sea
She was a perfect present for me.

Frances Clayden (10)
St Nicholas CE Primary School, Shepperton

The Sea

The sea rumbles and roars
Tumbles from side to side
Jumps up and down
Goes back and forth
Crashing upon the rocks
Landing on top of yellow sand
Rough and wet
Swiftly pulling away
Whoever dares to step in.

Shiza Khan (10)
St Nicholas CE Primary School, Shepperton

Rugby

Rugby is tough
Rugby is rough
Rugby means mud
That's the thing I love

On a cold Sunday morning
The team is yawning
We all soon wake up
That's the thing I love

Quite often it's raining
During our training
Rain, hail or shine
That's the thing I love

After the game
We'd all like the fame
Of scoring some tries
That's the thing I love.

Joe Spencer (10)
St Nicholas CE Primary School, Shepperton

A White Tiger

A white tiger is a . . .
Fierce hunter
Tail twitcher
Scary hisser
Loud growler
Stripy taker
Vicious killer
Lovely creature
Pictured feature
Meat eater
Lazy sleeper
Silent creeper.

Tia Gill (10)
St Nicholas CE Primary School, Shepperton

Tonight, Tonight

Tonight, tonight
    I'm going to have a fright with the bogey monster tucked in tight
He creeps up the stairs along the hallway, opens the door
And I see something slimy
That's why
Tonight, tonight
    I'm going to have a fright with the bogey monster tucked in tight

Tonight, tonight
    I'm going to have a fright with the bogey monster tucked in tight
He goes to sleep but I stay awake, for goodness sake I need a break
He wakes up in the middle of the night and we have
An enormous pillow fight
That's why
Tonight, tonight
    I'm going to have a fright with the bogey monster tucked in tight.

Paris Sweetland (9)
St Nicholas CE Primary School, Shepperton

Sharks

Sharks are fierce and mean
Swimming deep and unseen
Little fish run and hide
Don't show your fear deep inside

Divers beware under the waves
Sharks lay and wait in the caves
His shadow creeps along the sandy floor
Searching for his prey along the shore

Beady eyes never close
Razor-sharp teeth and pointed nose
Smooth and sleek, long and lean
Watch out, watch out, you've been seen.

George Scofield (10)
St Nicholas CE Primary School, Shepperton

The Leopard

Swift sprinter
Fierce fighter
Hard hitter
Berserk biter
Crushing carnivore
Treacherous tear
Shaky, shrilling noise
Glary glance
Piercing prey
Silent stance
Lightning look
Darting desire
Terrible teeth
Shaky, shrilling noise.

Lee Gardiner (10)
St Nicholas CE Primary School, Shepperton

Shark

S howing his big teeth
H unting for little fishes
A huge dinner
R acing along the seabed
K illing anything in its way.

Tom Epton (9)
St Nicholas CE Primary School, Shepperton

The Winter Fairy

Pinky-orangey
winter sky.
Winter's colours will
never die.
Sunlight, moonlight
April falls.
Clouds like candyfloss
in powderpuff balls.
Santa's doing his
part-time shift.
Galloping reindeer will
give him a lift.
Now my fairy work
is nearly done.
Gee, this winter's been
lots of fun!

Katherine Harper (10)
St Nicholas CE Primary School, Shepperton

Winter's Coming

The sun shines brightly,
Lakes shimmer,
Trees blow,
Lights dimmer,
Autumn leaves fall,
Until winter's call,
But someday the world,
Will be nothing at all.

Vanessa Matthews (10)
St Nicholas CE Primary School, Shepperton

Girls

Girls rule
Boys drool
Never fool
That's cool
Girls are the best
Never rest
On patrol
In control
Never weak
Like to speak
Always strong
Never wrong
Purple gowns
Boogie on down
They're on a roll
So let's rock 'n' roll.

Laura Tucker (10)
St Nicholas CE Primary School, Shepperton

A Dolphin's Mind

D eep sea divers
O pening eyes everywhere
L aughing all the way
P laying with his mates
H igh in the air
I n the deep sea
N othing it wants except me!

Cayleigh Irvine (9)
St Nicholas CE Primary School, Shepperton

Shark

S wift movers,
H unting groovers,
A nimal killers,
R acing blood spillers,
K illing fish dinners,
S harks are also good swimmers.

Thomas Miles (10)
St Nicholas CE Primary School, Shepperton

Monkey

M ile to get to that banana.
O nly a few more minutes.
N ow I can smell that banana.
K ick that tree down quick.
E r, I need that banana.
Y es, I have the skin but no banana.

Albert Olliffe (9)
St Nicholas CE Primary School, Shepperton

Vampire

B rilliant swift movers!
A ll night seeking blood!
T errific eyesight in the dark!

Callum Rowley (9)
St Nicholas CE Primary School, Shepperton

What Am I?

D ashing through the sea
O nly stopping to jump
L eaping up and down
P laying with its friend
H iding in the waves
I t slides on the beach
N ever stops.

Chloe Walkinshaw (9)
St Nicholas CE Primary School, Shepperton

My Cat

My cat is like a racing car,
But all cuddly and furry,
He eats his food all fast and quick,
He miaows and miaows,
Unless I cuddle him,
I love my cat, Tigger.

Hayley Strong (9)
St Nicholas CE Primary School, Shepperton

There Was A Man From Slida

There was a young man from Slida
who wasn't a very good glider
he twirled round and round
till he fell to the ground
he'd probably had too much cider!

Calum Gulvin (9)
St Nicholas CE Primary School, Shepperton

My Friend

My friend is short,
And at school is well taught.
She always wears a dress,
And is never in a mess.

She has blonde hair and blue eyes,
And nearly always cries.
She is nearly four,
And her mum and dad are definitely not poor!

She is very lucky,
And never gets mucky.
People adore her,
And she's called little Laura.

Lowri Chapman (9)
St Nicholas CE Primary School, Shepperton

Who Am I?

Nose like a giant hose
As huge as a house
A tail as skinny as a rope
Lives in the jungle
I have colossal ears
My skin is grey like metal
I eat delicious fruits
Enormous steps
Large eyes
Massive mouth

Who am I?

Alex Stabler (9)
St Nicholas CE Primary School, Shepperton

What Am I?

I am up in the sky
Where I see things fly
I sit in a brown nest
I am the best
I sing to my friends
As the twig eventually bends
I will give you a clue
I am bright blue
I am a cool creature
With very impressive features
My voice is powerful
I am very colourful
I can definitely be heard
I am a . . .

Elizabeth Voice (9)
St Nicholas CE Primary School, Shepperton

Fancy Fox

F earless fighter
A dventurous biter
N aughty neighbour
C hicken they favour
Y elling at her young

F antastic tongue
O utdoor creature
eX citing teacher.

Katy Hester (10)
St Nicholas CE Primary School, Shepperton

Lost

I'm all alone,
Everyone stares at me,
Maybe it's because I don't speak their language,
Maybe it's because of my colour,
I need a friend.

They think I'm different,
Just because I was moved from my beloved home,
They call me names,
They say I'm not welcome in their town.

I do not know where to turn,
I'm struggling,
I need a friend,
Maybe it's because I'm a refugee.

I'm lost!

Freja Rundle (10)
St Nicholas CE Primary School, Shepperton

It's A . . .

Silent glider,
Rule abider,
Swooping fast,
Very vast,
Goes on water,
Hates slaughter,
Loves being fed,
While in bed,
Likes being heard,
It's a . . .

Scott Brent Lancaster (10)
St Nicholas CE Primary School, Shepperton

My Strange Toy Cupboard

In my strange toy cupboard,
There are as weird things as can be,
Lions, leopards, tigers, dogs, cats and mice,
One day when I was playing, they all came to tea.

They made a giant mess,
Paw prints in the tea bags on the floor,
I hid the animals and tidied up the mess,
Then suddenly, Mum and Dad came through the door.

They came up to my room,
They were terribly impressed,
They put me in my cosy bed,
So that I could get my rest.

Ben Went (10)
St Nicholas CE Primary School, Shepperton

What Am I?

Slow eater,
good jumper,
milk guzzler,
lovely and furry,
soft as a feather,
glowing eyes,
purring fast,
doesn't growl,
faster than a Ferrari,
lays on a mat,
I am a . . . ?

Connor Herron (9)
St Nicholas CE Primary School, Shepperton

I Love Animals

I love animals big and small
I even help them when they fall

I have animals lots and lots
some I keep in little pots

I keep animals sick and well
and the ones I breed I have to sell

I race animals fast and slow
and all my horses like to tow

I help animals through the rough
but I think they are all pretty tough

I vet the animals when they're sick
and all my animals love to lick

I give animals lots of things
they all jump up when my bird sings

I share animals with friends
I am always upset when their life ends.

Tayler Fewster (9)
St Nicholas CE Primary School, Shepperton

It's A . . .

It lives in the blue sea
It's bigger than a tree
It squirts water out
From its little spout
They don't breathe in water
They don't have teeth at all
They have bigger eyes than marbles
And high-pitched singing calls.
It's a . . .

Tommy-Lee Gardner (9)
St Nicholas CE Primary School, Shepperton

Swan

Swift mover, graceful glider,
Men really admire her.

Easy to find in the night,
Because she's a glossy white.

She's got a bad temper,
With her babies she pampers.

She's a silent hider,
Her wings spread wider.

Alex Harrison (9)
St Nicholas CE Primary School, Shepperton

Football

The pitch is bright
The atmosphere's right
We're walking out of the stands,
Everyone can see their fans.
The whistle goes,
The atmosphere rose,
The ball hits the back of the net,
Now everyone's making a bet.

Elliott Hinds (9)
St Nicholas CE Primary School, Shepperton

Hip Hop

Hip hop hopping
Hipping to the hop
Don't stop to the rhythm
That'll make your body rock
'Cause me, the crew and my friends
Are gonna like to say, 'Yo! Yo!'

Declan Naylor (9)
St Nicholas CE Primary School, Shepperton

Sloth

Sloths are small, slow, pink animals,
With long, enormous tails.
They climb trees
With razor-sharp claws.
When they have clambered up the tree
They hang upside down and sleep. Zzzz.

Elliot Carter (9)
St Nicholas CE Primary School, Shepperton

Love

Love is good, love is great,
love is something to celebrate.
It broke my heart I'll never forgive it,
but it's still in my heart,
waiting to be opened once again.

James Parsonage (9)
St Nicholas CE Primary School, Shepperton

Books

B ooks are fun, books are sad
O ther books are naughty, some are true
O pen one up and feel the magic
K nowledge, information, illustration
S o take some advice and grab books now.

Dominic Hillman (9)
St Nicholas CE Primary School, Shepperton

The Wonderful Game

Football there's nothing better
Zidane, Henry, Ronaldo
Keepers, sweepers, the good old goal scorer
Prowling round the net waiting to pounce
To save the ball from going in the net
The fans go wild as the ball goes in
Not good for the ones who place the bet
Wenger and Fergie shouting
Letting us see their chewing gum
Thinking the other team are scum
Keane and Viera fouling each other
But not in front of their mother
Arsenal, Real Madrid
But there's only one team
That everyone knows, that's my team
St Joe's!

Pierce O'Connor (11)
St Teresa's RC First & Middle School & Nursery, Harrow Weald

Cheetah

A very fast creature,
Black spots are his feature,
Watching out for his prey,
Snorking in the long grass every day,
Twisting and turning,
With his stomach yearning,
And he really feels,
He really wants a delicious meal,
To brighten up his day!

He sees a deer,
Shivering with fear,
And starts to make a run for it,
The deer is fast and really fit,
But I'm afraid it's too fast for the cheetah so he sits.

Evlyne Oyedokun (11)
St Teresa's RC First & Middle School & Nursery, Harrow Weald

Seasons Hot And Seasons Cold

The new life season yes it's spring
When all the new birds love to sing
Daffodils all bright and yellow
Covering the bright green meadow.

Long summer days are hot and bright
Dark grey clouds are nowhere in sight
We're off to Spain we're on our way
We're off to Spain hooray, hooray!

Red, yellow and brown crispy leaves
Which have fallen off the trees
Hallowe'en is here, trick or treat?
They're waiting at the door
Trick or treat? Trick or treat?
Wanting sweets more and more.

Christmas is coming
Everyone is humming
Turkey dinners everywhere
People collecting for Christmas care.

Jamie Brogan (11)
St Teresa's RC First & Middle School & Nursery, Harrow Weald

My Tatty Trainers

My tatty trainers have walked a million miles
They are old, cool and smelly!
Like shining stars on my feet
Fast as a lion hunting for some meat.
I love my trainers because I have had them so long,
I feel like I'm king of the world and ever so strong!
My tatty trainers have walked a million miles.

Sean Matthews (11)
St Teresa's RC First & Middle School & Nursery, Harrow Weald

Sea

Deepest blue
And crashing waves,
Wonders inside
Its underwater caves,
Heaps of seaweed
Shells galore
Magical fish
That you would adore!
Mysterious secrets
That you'll never know,
Under the water
Where only fish go,
Sometimes it's scary
Living under the sea,
But most of the time,
You'll be as happy as can be!
Ferocious sharks
And whales so long,
They make noise
When they come along!
And that's my journey
Under the sea,
I hope you enjoy
Where I love to be!

Ailish Carolan (10)
St Teresa's RC First & Middle School & Nursery, Harrow Weald

My Dog

My loveable dog is the most incredible dog in the world
She is fantastic, fluffy and energetic
My dog has fur like a lion's mane
She jumps like a horse at Ascot
My dog makes me feel happy when I am down
She is like the best medicine anyone could have
My loveable dog, she makes me feel over the moon!

Michael Kennedy (10)
St Teresa's RC First & Middle School & Nursery, Harrow Weald

Winter

Winter is here hurrah, hurrah!
Snowmen are outside in the snow today,
My heart is beating as I watch the snow,
Children are playing near, far, high and low.

The snow is like a thick white blanket,
Cuddling the houses as the houses thank it,
I can see families huddling by the fire,
While the frozen snow gets higher and higher.

Winter fills me with brightness!
While the street lights fill the streets with lightness,
When it snows it is amazing I can't describe,
When it's winter it makes me feel so alive.

As the snow falls down it feels like Christmas is near,
I am so happy inside I have no fear,
Children with bright red faces are cheering and shouting,
While fluffy snow is mounting and mounting.

Snow makes me feel so good!
I wish it was snowing every day I wish it could,
Winter is really exciting, it really is,
People enjoy winter, especially kids,
The snow is settling hurrah! Hurrah!
Now we can go outside and play!

Shanice Thomas (11)
St Teresa's RC First & Middle School & Nursery, Harrow Weald

My Skateboard

Fast as anything,
Long, fast, bouncy,
As long as a dinosaur's neck,
As fast as a cheetah,
It makes me feel different,
Like a person that no one can see.
My skateboard.

Christy Casey (11)
St Teresa's RC First & Middle School & Nursery, Harrow Weald

The Circus

A great big circus tent,
Covered all over with stars,
Wonderful, big, humungous,
It sends me up to Mars!

Like a great big blanket thrown over some poles,
Stretching over the dreary ground,
Go in and see the circus ring,
And hear the brilliant sound.

See trapeze artists flying high,
Birds sliding down slides,
The ringmaster's big top hat,
And ponies giving rides.

Taste the sweet, soft candyfloss,
Maybe spin a plate,
Now the circus is finished,
Now it's getting late.

Rachel Cunniffe (11)
St Teresa's RC First & Middle School & Nursery, Harrow Weald

My Great Cats

My great cats
Jump around all the time
They're soft, cuddly and fast
They're like lions hunting their prey
They're like cheetahs chasing some animals
They make me feel slow
Like a racing rhino that can't move
My great cats
Remind me how great life is.

Danny McIntyre (10)
St Teresa's RC First & Middle School & Nursery, Harrow Weald

Lulu

My little sister Lulu
She is five years old
In her high heels and tutu
She sparkles pink and gold

Her hair is blonde, her eyes are green
She acts like she's the best
Like we're her servants, she's the queen
Who cares about the rest?

Barbie dolls and teddy bears
Are her favourite toys
She maybe in reception class
But still gets all the boys!

She always steals Mum's lipstick
And smears it on her face
She wraps herself in jewellery
Frills and fur and lace

She likes to read me stories
Although they make no sense
I have to praise her at the end
And keep up the pretence

That all she says is wonderful
And wise and clear and funny
'Cause if I don't she'll just get mad
And hit me with her bunny!

Although she may annoy me
And makes me feel quite blue
She's my sister and I love her
I wouldn't swap her, would you?

Holly Cook (10)
St Teresa's RC First & Middle School & Nursery, Harrow Weald

The Great Game

The whistle blows
And off we go!
People cheering high
And low.
'Cross the field the ball will flow,
The players put on such a great show.

There they go from end to end,
Between the players the ball they send.
At last it flies up in the air,
The crowd cheer!
Will it go in?
Their hearts are beating like alarm clocks,
Their faces are full of shock.
Will It go In?
It's not a goal but the players will still try to win!

Luke Burke (10)
St Teresa's RC First & Middle School & Nursery, Harrow Weald

Snow

The cold, white snow
Is white and beautiful
Small, fluffy, cold and wet
Like a falling cloud covering the land
For grip we put down yellow, golden sand
It makes me feel excited and cold
Like I'm in a white, wonderful world
It's special snow, we throw it and jump in it.

Jordan O'Neill (11)
St Teresa's RC First & Middle School & Nursery, Harrow Weald

My Dog, Pixie

My dog, Pixie
An extraordinary pet,
Who's small but cuddly
And she's never been to the vet.
She can be naughty but sweet,
And she loves to have a special treat.
Her fur is curly black,
And her paw prints make a twisting track.
Pixie is very playful,
And loves to eat a tray full.
When she's upset her tail goes between her legs,
Her paws go up and for forgiveness is what she begs.
At the end of the day,
She curls up and doesn't want to play.
She goes to her bed and goes to sleep,
And dreams of tomorrow and what will be her treat.

Keri McEvoy (11)
St Teresa's RC First & Middle School & Nursery, Harrow Weald

Tooth Fairy

In the night it sneaks, searching for those who've lost their teeth
Not daring to make a sound
They're gentle and fly around
Beneath the pillow the tooth lies waiting
Waiting but no one replies
Until in the dead of night
When the tooth fairy comes everything's going to be all right
Under the pillow it glistens gold
A coin is left just like I was told.

Joanna Lewis (11)
St Teresa's RC First & Middle School & Nursery, Harrow Weald

My Brother Elliot

My brother Elliot was born nine years ago,
The torture, the torture being with him alone,
Small, daring, funny,
When he's asleep he's like a snoring little bunny.
When he is awake he plays with his mates,
But when he is back he's muddy for goodness sake!
Sometimes he is kind, sometimes he is naughty,
And even sometimes he calls me Shorty.

My brother Elliot is as strong as a lion,
Cool as a cucumber, but loud as a siren.
Even though he's annoying, maybe a little impolite,
Our love for both of us is as strong as a knight.
Our love will never break down,
Even though I sometimes frown.
We're united together, strong as a shield,
Our love grows like crops in a rich field.

Fraser Simpson (11)
St Teresa's RC First & Middle School & Nursery, Harrow Weald

My Brother Tyler

My brother Tyler
Was born six years ago
Small, mighty and annoying yes I know!
But as mighty as a lion
As gentle as a mouse!
I love him to bits in and outside the house.
My love for him is like my love for football
My brother Tyler's so special to me
He reminds me of how my life used to be.

Treston McKenzie (11)
St Teresa's RC First & Middle School & Nursery, Harrow Weald

My Pet Ozzy

My pet Ozzy is a bird,
He can fly around the world,
He walks on my head,
He tickles my hand,
But he just hates playing with the sand,
He's fast, he's noisy, he's mighty and strong,
He tweaks with the music all day long.

Ozzy is like a lion roaring around,
With his cheerful little birdie sound.
He makes me feel as happy as can be,
To know that someone is beside with me,
I love Ozzy with all my heart,
I can tell you something,
He's really smart,
He's fast, he's furious, he's like a car,
My pet Ozzy is a star.

Tamara Joanes Dias (10)
St Teresa's RC First & Middle School & Nursery, Harrow Weald

My Dad's House

My dad's house
Made of bricks and painted white,
Warm, fun and cool
Like a magic kingdom in the sky,
Like my favourite toy shop,
It makes me feel happy and safe,
Like a prince in a castle
My dad's house,
A great place to be.

Simon Teer (10)
St Teresa's RC First & Middle School & Nursery, Harrow Weald

Boys And Girls In Class

Why do boys and girls in class,
Choose to throw words just like glass?
Is it part of a fashion?
Can I ask you,
'Where is the compassion?'

Are you proud of your behaviour?
Making someone feel they are in danger,
Bruises heal, the marks go away,
Words scare, the marks will stay.

The boys and girls in class,
Make me feel sad,
Make me mad,
Why do they like making me feel so bad?

It is not so hard to be kind,
Try it and you will find,
Peace of mind,
Boys and girls in class.

Samantha Vanderputt (10)
St Teresa's RC First & Middle School & Nursery, Harrow Weald

My Sister

My lovely Lucy
Born in December. The month of joy and love
Cool, clever, cute
Like a Valentine's rose
Like a barking sea
She makes me feel proud when she's with me
My lovely Lucy
A kind, loving sister.

Chantelle Frampton (10)
St Teresa's RC First & Middle School & Nursery, Harrow Weald

Seasons

Spring is when buds come out,
Baby animals hear them shout.
Here comes Easter with chocolate eggs,
Little chicks with tiny legs.

Summer is hot and fun,
With the burning, boiling sun.
It's a time to see all your friends,
It feels like it never ends.

Autumn is when leaves fall off trees
And when animals go for a sleep.
The plants go all brown and dreary,
Hopefully winter's here: very nearly.

Now winter's here, it's cold and icy,
It bites your lip like something spicy.
Come on now it's Christmas time!
Hear the Christmas bells that chime.

Seasons do come and go,
Now it's time to play in the snow!

Abbie Carey (10)
St Teresa's RC First & Middle School & Nursery, Harrow Weald

My Great Mum

My great mum,
Who brings me light every morning,
She's a loveable, happy and helpful person
She's like a warm, cuddly cushion
My mum is a bright shooting star in the night sky
She will be there wherever I go
My great mum
Reminds me of what love is.

Lauren Lehane (10)
St Teresa's RC First & Middle School & Nursery, Harrow Weald

Purring Pussycat

(Dedicated to my cat, Watson)

I have a cat
Who loves to cuddle
And when he's as happy
As a bright summer's day
He purrs.
His glossy fur coat
Is as soft as silk
As dark as midnight
As fluffy as clouds
When I stroke him
And cuddle him lots
What do you think he does?
He purrs
He purrs
He purrs.

Sarah Innes (11)
St Teresa's RC First & Middle School & Nursery, Harrow Weald

My Mum

The best mum in the world
Huggable, loveable, friendly
Has hair like the night sky
Soft as a panther
She makes me feel like I am the best
Like a king on a throne
She reminds me of an animal
Looking after her young.

Tristan Thomas
St Teresa's RC First & Middle School & Nursery, Harrow Weald

I Know Someone That Is . . .

I know someone that is . . .

Clever, funny and sensitive,
Is as happy as the sun,
Is as cute as a kitten,
As sweet as sugar.

They can be . . .
As grumpy as a gorilla,
As cheeky as a chimpanzee
And this person is me!

Rebecca Hine (11)
St Teresa's RC First & Middle School & Nursery, Harrow Weald

My Teacher

My teacher,
is very old, about a million and two,
wrinkly, stiff, old,
as old as the moon,
as wrinkly as a tree,
she makes me feel upset that she teaches me.
As sad as a man who's lost his favourite tree,
my teacher reminds me how old you can be.

Raymond Cullis (10)
St Teresa's RC First & Middle School & Nursery, Harrow Weald

Cadbury's Creme Egg

Cadbury's Creme Egg
It's like a massive sweet ball rolling around your mouth.
Swirling, curling, whirling
A round ball like the Earth.
It makes me feel alive
As it swirls inside your mouth
You know the best place to get it is in the south.
The ream of cream whips inside your mouth.
Reminds us of how it would be like
Without the Cadbury's Creme Egg.
The outside of the chocolate
Is tied to your tongue and your teeth.
That's the lovely Cadbury's Creme Egg.

Callum Murchun (11)
St Teresa's RC First & Middle School & Nursery, Harrow Weald

The Shadowlord

The Shadowlord, he who lurks in the dark,
More fearsome than the fiercest shark,
His terrifying bloodshot eyes,
Which he uses to spy,
His next unlucky victim, who dared to wander away,
Will soon become his prey,
He strikes, quieter than a mouse,
Although he is larger than a house,
He shall devour you with massive jaws,
Tearing you in half with clashing claws,
Always keep on your guard, don't wander around,
Or you shall soon be found . . .

Jake Embley (10)
St Teresa's RC First & Middle School & Nursery, Harrow Weald

The Park

We go to the park,
When it's not dark,
Made for friends to play,
Lots of things to do and say,
We go running and jumping,
We often sing,
We are very loud,
Under the clouds,
We look so small,
Playing football,
The mums come,
Like a rumbling drum,
We leave one by one,
Until there is none.

Michael Baggs (10)
St Teresa's RC First & Middle School & Nursery, Harrow Weald

My Pet Snowbell

My pet Snowbell is a West Highland terrier,
Cuddly like a hairy cushion
Her face is beautiful, cute, happy

Out in the garden she jumps for joy,
Playing, having the time of her life.
She keeps me company and cheers me up.

My pet Snowbell who is a West Highland terrier
Is the friendliest dog I've ever had.

Laila Sheridan (10)
St Teresa's RC First & Middle School & Nursery, Harrow Weald

My Wonderful Holiday

My wonderful holiday was full of fun
With all the things to do
Under the sun

The warm sea
Right up to my knee
There is nowhere else I would rather be

The golden ground right under my feet
Spread for miles
Ever so neat

Running and screaming the children would play
Telling their mothers
They all want to stay

The seagulls dance around the sky
As I rise to my feet
I would sit right back down
On my seat.

Natasha Sendanayake (10)
St Teresa's RC First & Middle School & Nursery, Harrow Weald

Twin Brothers

They're double trouble
They make fun and mischief
In the house

But when the whistle blows
In a Gaelic match
They catch, kick, score goals.

People stop and stare
Watching their fabulous feet.
They're unbelievable
There's no doubt about that.

But really they make lots of mischief.

Sean Derbyshire (10)
St Teresa's RC First & Middle School & Nursery, Harrow Weald

The Sun

I love summer
With the beautiful sun,
It always hangs around me
It makes my life such fun.

I love the sun
It shines in my face,
It travels everywhere
But never lands in space.

The sun is a gigantic ball
But hopefully it will never fall,
It comes at any time of year
There is no need to *fear!*

Daniel Clarke (10)
St Teresa's RC First & Middle School & Nursery, Harrow Weald

Things I Like

I like the winter breeze
Blowing in my face
I like the autumn trees
Amongst the open space

I like the sound of the ocean
It wraps its waves around me
I like the smoothness of sun lotion
And the sound of the bumblebee

I like the sunshine
And how it brightens my day
Making me feel so fine
As I go along my way.

Bethany Pelling (11)
St Teresa's RC First & Middle School & Nursery, Harrow Weald

Crocodile

The fierce, furious crocodile,
Lies deep beneath the water,
Always full of strength.

It has long, rough skin
With green, scary eyes.
It has a gigantic tail,
As long as me
It's big and powerful,
Full of strength.

It's like a secret agent
On a secret mission.
Sneaking up behind its prey,
The fish are terrified
Gulp!
He swims away
With a tummy full.

The fierce, furious crocodile,
Lies deep beneath the water,
Always full of strength.

Anthony Lewis (11)
St Teresa's RC First & Middle School & Nursery, Harrow Weald

The Bogeyman

The bogeyman, huge and nasty,
lurks in your cupboard,
waiting for children to scare.
He takes them away
and bakes his prey,
eating them with his slimy lips,
mean and angry.

Ryan Cox (11)
St Teresa's RC First & Middle School & Nursery, Harrow Weald

The Night

The night is late
Yet I am awake
This is my first
So let me cast
The sweet memories of the night
Which are so bright.

Up in the sky
Sparkling so high
Lies the twinkling stars
It seems so near yet so far.

The sky is slightly dark
And it makes a mark
In my childish heart

The beautiful moon is gleaming
So I am feeling
Joyful and fine
To see birds go flying

The night is late
Yet I am awake
This is my last
So let it go fast

As I close my eyes
I feel as the wind flies
Slowly
Very slowly.

Anita Anthony (11)
St Teresa's RC First & Middle School & Nursery, Harrow Weald

Light

Light, a beautiful creation made by God.
We use it every day in the early morning to the darkest night.
The sun is the largest light source we could ask for.
Thank you for the beautiful light.

James Okeyemi (11)
St Teresa's RC First & Middle School & Nursery, Harrow Weald

Me

As long as I'm alive
I will sometimes be myself,
But sometimes someone else
But probably just me.

I have blue, twinkling eyes
Which would win any prize,
I have a cheeky smile
As big as the Nile.

I am a great friend
I won't drive you round the bend,
I am gentle and nice
Like sugar and spice.

I can be a great help
But might make you yelp,
I am very funny
Like a silly bunny.

And that's that
So take a look
And you will see
That this is me.

Grace Barber (11)
St Teresa's RC First & Middle School & Nursery, Harrow Weald

Winter

Cold as ice
But still as nice
Beautiful to see
As nice as can be
Winter.

Earan Grey (10)
St Teresa's RC First & Middle School & Nursery, Harrow Weald

Flowers

Flowers, they're like a new painting
Which has vibrant colours
The colours of the rainbow
The scents, nothing other than flowers!
Flowers they fill you with happiness and joy
More than anything else.
They are like a story
Some have long beginnings and short ends
Flowers, some are short, some are tall
Some are big, some are small, but overall
The colours are the best.

Christian Fraser-Williams (11)
St Teresa's RC First & Middle School & Nursery, Harrow Weald

Pizza

Pizza
The best food ever.
As hot as the rising sun, yummy, delicious, tasty.
Like a large, round cheesy disc.
Like a little slice of heaven.
My mouth starts watering.
Pizza
With delight when I take the first bite.
Wow! I'm hungry
Mmmmm! That's nice.

Nathanael Munir (10)
St Teresa's RC First & Middle School & Nursery, Harrow Weald

Gloom!

I'm sitting down in my gloom,
In the corner of my room.
Sitting on my battered suitcase
With oval tears running down my face.
Looking over in my mind
For an explanation I might find.
Hitting my head against a wall
In hope that I might fall.
Sitting in the corner of my room
In the depth of my *gloom!*

Christina Baker (11)
St Teresa's RC First & Middle School & Nursery, Harrow Weald

Winter

Winter is here again
Here comes the snow and the rain
Icy, bitter winds
Like an artist who sprayed the world white
Like a whiteboard waiting to flow
I'm as cold as an ice block
Wishing I could stop the clock.

Jordan Carroll (10)
St Teresa's RC First & Middle School & Nursery, Harrow Weald

The Ice Cream Rap!

Ice cream on a hot summer's day,
Make the heat go away,
When my pudding's much too hot,
Ice cream makes it not!

On its own it cools my throat,
In the sun or on a boat,
I still like ice cream in the wintertime,
To go without would be a crime!

My favourite ice cream is flavoured with toffee,
Don't give me anything flavoured with coffee,
Vanilla goes with everything,
Ice cream with ginger makes my mouth sting!

Eating ice cream can be really cool,
Go to a parlour and sit on a stool,
Order a sundae,
Even on a Monday!

Making ice cream is as easy as pie,
To go without you'll want to die,
Mix in all things nice,
Then eat as cold as ice!

It'll rot your teeth that's for sure,
Though you'll love it so much you'll be begging for more,
You'd be lost without it,
You'll lose teeth through it!

That concludes our ice cream rap,
Now you've got that tap, tap, tap.
Ice cream, ice cream, ice cream
It just makes you want to *scream!*

Jemima Davey (9)
Twickenham Prep School

The Midnight Flyer

Deep in the dark,
There stands a spark,
A little man in the dark,
With a little mark,
He flies in the night.

He gives people a little fright,
He never gives a bite,
He pulls you very tight,
He always keeps a crystal ball
It always gives a call.

He will never bounce a ball,
He is also very tall,
So mind him,
He comes to you in the night.

Nikki Thind (8)
Twickenham Prep School

Morning, Midday And Evening

Morning is the newborn child,
Squealing and crying,
Can be warm can be mild,
The night is dying.

Midday is the lion cub,
Twisting and turning in its play,
Suncream out, everyone rub,
Everyone wanting the sun to stay.

Evening is the snake,
Slithering over the sky,
No one awake,
Nothing open, not even an eye.

Victoria Barnes (10)
Twickenham Prep School

Sweets! Sweets!

Liquorice, a black, chewy substance,
Toffee, a golden brown sticky lump,
Sherbet, a white, fizzy powder
And fudge, a brown, malleable block.

Sweets! Sweets!
Chewing, sucking, licking,
All day long,
Slurping sweets so scrummy.

Lollipops, delicious solid balls on a stick,
Jelly beans, fruity, bouncy beans,
Gobstoppers, big, round balls
And jelly babies, chewy, fruity babies.

Sweets! Sweets!
Lovely, scrumptious things,
But there's one thing missing,
Chocolate of course!

Louisa Bolton (10)
Twickenham Prep School

Cluedo

In a castle far away, many years ago,
Lived some people named Miss Scarlet,
Mrs White, Mrs Peacock, Colonel Mustard,
Professor Plum, Reverend Green
And the master, the master of the house.
That night it was silent,
So silent you could hear someone's feet
Get out a dagger and stab someone!
Then you could hear them go back to their room,
Then it was silent again.
It was midnight so no one woke up with morning light.
No one knew who killed who,
Not even me.

Alicia Gumpert (8)
Twickenham Prep School

What Happened That Night . . .

It was midnight at Slimmingdale,
As the full moon shone
And the wind was blowing a gale,
A shadow appeared from behind a tree.

It looked at the bus stop,
With its shabby paintwork
And then at the houses in a row.

It scanned them and automatically it came
To our house.
It gloomily walked forward
And climbed through an open window.

I was fast asleep in bed
Cuddling Ted (my toy bear).

I suddenly heard rasping breath,
Getting closer and closer.
I looked up into the gloom
And there was that haunting figure,
Leaning over me.

I'll never forget that night,
When I had that horrible,
Indescribable fright!

Jasmine Swan (10)
Twickenham Prep School

A Mystery Murder

Someone's been murdered!
I wonder who.
The window's been creaking
Who could it be?
I wonder who,
Who could it be?
But someone's been
Murdered.

Nidhi Puri (7)
Twickenham Prep School

The Year 3000

The sky is vicious violet,
The clouds are glorious green,
The treetops are brilliant blue,
The brightest I've ever seen.

Cars are furiously flying,
A few feet off the ground,
The noise is giving me a headache,
Making a strange sizzling sound.

I'll go to my room and rest my head
And hopefully sleep for a tiny bit,
I blow the candles smoothly and softly,
Now the candles are no longer lit.

I must sleep here and now,
While the world continues on its unpredictable path,
My eyelids shut slowly but surely
And suddenly I hear my mum's faint laugh.

Jessica Manning (11)
Twickenham Prep School

My Family

I love my mum she is cool and fun,
I love my dad he's never mean or bad,
I love my sis, even though she goes *hiss,*
I love my brother because he's like my mother.

Edward Smith (9)
Twickenham Prep School

The Bullying Bee

Butterflies flutter in the sky,
Twinkle, twinkle up so high,
Then the *bullying bee* buzzes and spoils their fun
As he points to the stinger on his bum!
He hovers and tears, buzzes and scares
Then the moment of truth finally comes when he leaves
And all the butterflies are dead on the floor
And the *bullying bee* sets out for more!

Now the *bullying bee* thought to himself
If I can take on butterflies, why not the horses in the field over there?
So the horses, oh the poor horses were another victim of
The *bullying bee*
So he pulled and tugged and was never intending to give them a hug.
So the *bullying bee* left triumphant once again but then he thought,
The horses are too easy for me, so I will go to the one place where
No one ever comes out alive!

So the *bullying bee* goes very far to the cave of the *bull!*
The strongest animal in the land.
He goes in, the *bull* is asleep, he really tries not to make a creak.
Then suddenly a stone falls and makes a clatter
The bull wakes up, the bee attacks
Then the *bull* hit the bee with the ring on his nose and knocked
The *bullying bee* out.
Then the *bull* knew that what he did was very wrong
And stayed by the bee's side until he woke up.
When the bee woke up he felt completely different,
He did not want to sting or tear or scare, but be friends with everyone
So, he never did anything like that again.
Hooray!

Charlotte Smith (10)
Twickenham Prep School

Spaghetti, Spaghetti

Spaghetti, spaghetti
Let's not forgetti,
That spaghetti,
Is wonderfully trunketti!
If appears on your plate,
It isn't just fate,
For spaghetti,
Is pasta confetti!

Spaghetti, spaghetti,
You can just about betti,
That spaghetti
Will tame a large yeti!
But, spaghetti, spaghetti
You must never regretti
Just how much we rely on
Spaghetti!

Lorn Jackson (10)
Twickenham Prep School

My Cat

Hobbs is our cat
And he's really quite fat.
He got stuck in a door
And miaowed for more.
We all shout hooray
For he's stuck there all day,
So give him a clap
For he'll come out quite flat.

Jake Gorridge (9)
Twickenham Prep School

The Cautious Cat
And The Mindless Mouse

A black cat prowls
From roof to roof, disguising itself
As the deep, dark, purply-blue midnight sky.
Silence, then its ears twitch
Its eyes glimmer, it sharpens its claws
Silently, then it crouches down to wait.
A dark silhouette appears on the scene.
Then the cat pounces.
Its teeth manage to catch the pink tail
Disappearing down the chimney.
The cat picks it up and soon
The only thing left is a small pink tail
And some bones scattered around.

Tove Hubbard (9)
Vaughan First & Middle School

The Sea

Near a sea
I hear a splash

A splash of happiness
and lightness.

My heart feels the love
and laughter

The sea fills me with
wonderful feelings.

The sea is a loving place
it makes me feel that I have love around me.

Just remember the sea is there for everyone.

Anushka Ahmad-D'Mello (9)
Vaughan First & Middle School

It Was So Quiet That . . .

It was so quiet that I could hear a worm munching through a ripe
apple inside a packed lunch box.
It was so quiet that I could hear the clouds swiftly moving in the air,
It was so quiet that I could hear a footballer celebrating his goal,
It was so quiet that I could hear an Alsatian dog walking on the
soft grass,
It was so quiet that I could hear a coin rattling on the floor,
It was so quiet that I could hear someone's hair being cut inside
a barbershop,
It was so quiet that I could hear a paper bag rustling in the wind,
It was so quiet that I could hear someone scribbling in his notebook,
It was so quiet that I could hear someone turning the pages of a book,
It was so quiet that I could hear water dripping in the sink,
It was so quiet that I could hear the engine starting outside,
It was so quiet that I could hear the head teacher marching outside
the classroom,
It was so quiet that I could hear the clock ticking as the time goes on,
It was so quiet that I could hear my sister listening to some music on
headphones,
It was so quiet that I could hear the creak of the door opening.

Hary Ilanko (10)
Vaughan First & Middle School

All The Children

The time? The time? The time?
It's just turned half-past nine
All the children go out to play
Hopefully it will be a bright sunny day.
They play on swings, they play on the slide
Whatever they do they do it with pride.

Victoria Body (9)
Vaughan First & Middle School

Ayesha Tright

Have you heard the story of Ayesha Tright?
She was always getting in a fight
One day Ayesha thought that she might just go
Away to a sunny delight.
When her plane was up in flight
She started to get quite uptight
An air hostess thought she'd stolen
Some money from a lad whose arms she'd broken
Ayesha got mad, Ayesha screamed
Ayesha threw a tantrum, she was full of steam
Ayesha was under a lot of stress
Now that she was under arrest
The air hostess loses the fight
She's never going on another flight
She's covered in bruises
All because of Ayesha Tright
Now you've heard the story of Ayesha Tright
Don't you ever get uptight.

Shamima Ali (10)
Vaughan First & Middle School

Acrostic

A crostic poems, I
C an't see the point of sta
R ting each line
O ff with a letter in a word or
S entence, I think it's s
T upid
I' d rather be eating cu
C umber sandwiches!

Brian Greene (7)
Vaughan First & Middle School

Me And A Cat Named Boo

The best friend in the world
Is my cat Boo
She always follows me around,
Even into the loo!

We play lots of games together,
Like hide-and-seek and tag
But her favourite one
Is sitting in a bag!

She likes sitting on the window sill,
In the midday heat,
Sneering at the fat tabby
Just across the street!

She fitted so well,
When first I held her
In my hand,
A tiny ball of grey fur.

Oh how she scratched
And marked my arm
When a sudden movement
Caused great alarm.

But now she is bigger,
Bolder and brave
Dogs have masters,
My cat has a slave!

We'll travel the world,
Have adventures galore,
When we get home
We'll go again for more.

Me and Boo,
Boo and me,
Like pizza and chips,
Some things are meant to be.

Samia Siddiqi (9)
Vaughan First & Middle School

I Wish I Had A Pony

I wish I had a pony
with a soft, white mane
he'd hang out in the stable
Cane would be his name.

I wish I had a pony
with big blue eyes
who wakes up in the morning
when the sun starts to rise.

I wish I had a pony
with a shiny brown tail
he'd look at the sky
to see the clouds sail

I wish I had a pony
with quite a lot of friends
who's good at finding locations
and turning round bends.

I wish I had a pony
who eats apple pies
would go under the shade
when there are sunny skies.

Karishma Tailor (10)
Vaughan First & Middle School

Run!

Run down town,
Run up and down
Run to the shops,
Run to buy an ice pop.
Run to the market,
Run to get a basket,
Run to buy a loaf of bread,
'Run to buy some butter,' Granny said.
Run what?
Run where?
Run to buy some underwear
Run to Mum's,
Run to Dad's,
Run and try to not go mad.
Run to the charity shop to buy a suit so shiny,
Mustn't laugh it isn't funny,
Run to buy some posh clothes,
Run to get a tissue for my runny nose,
Run to my comfy settee,
Run to make myself a cup of tea.

Layla Alami (10)
Vaughan First & Middle School

Untitled

The owls flew deep into the sky
Their eyes opened wide.
The trees blew and swayed constantly
The moon shone in the darkness.
The wind howled like wolves.
Soon the mornings appeared
And the sun rose.

Sarah Key (8)
Whiteheath Junior School

My Heart

Somewhere down, deep down inside,
There is a light, a path, a guide.
Everyone has one, I have mine,
Although it seems that I lose it sometimes.
I ask myself, just what could this be?
My blood, my skin, the real me.
But somewhere down, deep down inside,
I know this thing's not just my guide.
It is a bar, a bar of gold,
Though not the kind that you can hold.
This gold it is so close to me,
This gold and I were meant to be.
Bright gold it is, so pure, so clear,
It protects me from all cruelty and fear
This gold it was the very start,
Indeed this gold, it is my heart.

Caroline Cousins (9)
Whiteheath Junior School

Flames Of Fire

Flames of fire,
Rise as spirit,
Revealing true vision,
Showing strength of the holy light.

Flames of fire,
Lights the darkness,
Destroys the devil,
Protects the angel.

Flames of fire,
Drop as dead,
Ashes remain
And the cold chill returns.

Nehal Doshi (9)
Whiteheath Junior School

Nothing

When I lost someone very dear to me
There was nothing to grab a hold of,
Nothing to cling to, to steady me,
Nothing to dry my eyes on.

When I lost someone very dear to me
There was nothing to stop the pain,
Nothing to untie the knot in my heart,
Nothing to reassure me.

When I lost someone very dear to me
My nights of grief were endless,
My days were sorrow and stormy clouds,
There was nothing . . . no one . . .
When I lost someone very dear to me.

Georgia Russell (10)
Whiteheath Junior School

Whoops!

Whoops! Oh no I slipped
Now I've just got pipped,
I was just at the finish line
Now the trophy is not mine!

I guess I got second place
But that's not good enough for my pace
Now I've nicked his car key
'Cause he nicked the race from me!

Carl Pullem (10)
Whiteheath Junior School

Colours Of The World

Blue is rushing in the sea
Blue is in the sky
Blue is everything inside me
When the night says goodbye

Red is fire in the night
Red is what sets our world alight
Red is fierce. Red is strong
Red in the morning, when the moon has shone

Yellow is what makes up our world
Yellow is a story never to be told
Yellow light, yellow bright
Yellow shining in the moonlight

Green the grass, the leaves, the trees
Green flowers under buzzing bees
Green is all around us so
Leave everything green alone to grow.

Jessica Leese (9)
Whiteheath Junior School

Stallion

Stallion of the enchanted park,
The racer of eagles
As strong as an arc.

Stallion of the wild flower field,
The power of an ox,
Defends like a shield.

Stallion of the peaceful meadow,
As fierce as a sword,
As swift as an arrow.

Stallion of the silent moor,
The peace of an angel
And a heart so pure.

Christopher Musgrave (10)
Whiteheath Junior School

The Tennis Ball

I am yellow and round.
Spend most of my life on the ground.
I bring fun and joy to many kids on the block
Especially when they want a knock.

They throw me into the air
And serve me into the net.
Phew, what a relief!
I've avoided that return.
But! Uh-oh here we go again
This time over the net
And smack into the corner
And ouch! Back again.

Wow, what a rally!
The crowds are cheering loudly
What a relief we've got a winner.

Now I can rest again
In my safe ball basket
With my special friends.

Robyn Wetteland (8)
Whiteheath Junior School

Summer

Summer is a season in the year,
You might hear the wind whistle in your ear.
The sun is bright, children are playing,
People are laying on a blanket in the garden.
The ice cream man's noise,
The children are playing with toys.
Flowers are sprouting,
Some people go for an outing.
Summer is a wonderful time of the year.

Christopher Demosthenous (9)
Whiteheath Junior School

Leopard

Stalking through the long green grass
on the African plains.
A leopard is
hunting for her prey.

She leaps, jumps and pounces
onto the male gazelle.
She bites it with her teeth like daggers
for she has caught her meal.

When she has finished eating
she will climb a tree.
Lay on a trunk and sleep
for three days.

When she wakes up
she will hunt again.
Maybe a zebra, wildebeest or an antelope.
Who knows? It's a leopard's life!

Kirstie Guildford (7)
Whiteheath Junior School

The Monster's Disco

Late at night
When you're asleep
The monsters come out
And party deep

Frankenstein does the cha-cha-cha
But Count Dracula does much more
All the ghosts are doing the spooks
And the werewolf is on the dance floor.

George Leen (9)
Whiteheath Junior School

The Sea And Beach

In winter,
The sea and beach are fun.
But when the sun sets,
You can bet,
It will be time to run.

In spring,
The sea and beach are fun.
We collect shells by the shore,
But we always see much more
And then it's time to run.

In summer,
The sea and beach are fun.
We go for a dip,
Then we drip,
Before it's time to run.

In autumn,
The sea and beach are fun.
With the wind in our hair,
I'm blown everywhere,
But then it's time to run.

Dominic Apuzzo (7)
Whiteheath Junior School

The Future

The future, the future, I want to see the future,
Do they laugh and cry, do they live and die?

Are there robots there? Do they breathe fresh air?
Do they go to school? Is what they wear cool?
The future, the future, I want to see the future!

The school of the future!

Verity Ball (10)
Whiteheath Junior School

My Dad Is Fun

My dad is fun,
I'm glad I am his son.
We play all the time
Rain or shine.

We go to the park
And have a lark,
We don't go home
Till it's dark.

Danny Lewis (8)
Whiteheath Junior School

My Ice Cream

Sticky, frozen ice cream, slipping everywhere.
As slimy as a warm, rough, crunchy cone
With a sharp, pointed peak, just waiting to be eaten.
You can get it in chocolate chip, rainbow sherbet,
Chocolate mint, vanilla and strawberry.
Yum! Yum! Yum!

Candice Devine (9)
Whiteheath Junior School

Ice Cream

Ice cream is as runny as water
As tall as a phone
Super selling, special
Ice cream's from a supreme shop.
Cracking, crunchy,
Curling, colourful shell.
Gob-smacking!
Drip, drip, drop . . .
It's melted!

Jared Smart (8)
Whiteheath Junior School

The Beautiful Butterfly

The butterfly, the beautiful butterfly
is as delicate as a rose.
You will never catch this butterfly.

Hovering over the blue and deep sea
the butterfly would fly over to me!
The most beautiful butterfly now swoops by,
now and forever nothing will stop it!
You could stare at the butterfly all day long.

The magnificent butterfly
is as beautiful as the ocean.

The beautiful butterfly
is as light as a feather.

The beautiful butterfly swooped by,
flying and fluttering in the starlit sky.
Passing shiny pebbles,
standing out forever in the moonlit sky.

Lauren Wilson (9)
Whiteheath Junior School

The Melting Ice Cream

The ice cream was in the sun
waiting to be licked.
I came along and licked it,
it was lovely and thick.
I bit some of the cornet
it was crunchy as a biscuit.

The ice cream was as cold as snow.
There were six sticky scoops of ice cream
and it was delicious and
I ate it all!

Ciara Murphy (9)
Whiteheath Junior School

Aeroplane

Take-off, first slow then fast and at last we're in the air!
From the window everything is small,
The school, the house, even Big Ben!
Look here comes dinner. *Urgh!* It tastes horrible!
Hey look we're over the sea.
Whaaah! A baby's crying!
Oh no, I won't be able to go to sleep
So I'll watch the movie instead.

Billy Stark (9)
Whiteheath Junior School

Birds

Red as a robin,
Kingfisher-blue,
Grey as a seagull,
Black as a blackbird,
Brown as a wren,
Bullfinch-pink,
Yellow as a siskin,
Blue as a blue tit.

James Skinner (10)
Whiteheath Junior School

The Snail

Snails are like slugs with a shell as their home.
Sometimes their slime looks like foam.
They can live in your garden under the hedge.
They also like it on your window ledge.
They have a shell a bit like a stone.
But definitely not an ice cream cone!

Emma Watson (9)
Whiteheath Junior School

The Bite

The sandwich can be eaten but only if you try,
No one gets through the lunch box, you'll see why.
The chocolates will see you first,
They'll tempt you till you eat them.
But at the bottom you will see a sandwich
That has lettuce as green as the grass,
Tomatoes as red as a rose, the bread as brown
As a piece of chocolate.
You will be too by the time you get to
The sandwich!

Rebecca Gyetvai (9)
Whiteheath Junior School

Noisy Traffic

One wonky wheelchair wobbling wildly
Two tatty Toyotas taming
Three thrilling Thunderbirds throbbing
Four Ford Fiestas flaming
Five fast Ferraris flitting frantically
Six slow Sierras sleeping
Seven super Subarus skidding
Eight Aston Martins still living
Nine Nissans driving around
Ten Toyotas talking.

Emma Pereira (11)
Wood End Park Community School

In The Canteen

Children eating,
Children greeting,
Children dreaming, dreaming, dreaming

Children chomping,
Children chatting,
Children chewing, chewing, chewing

Children sleeping,
Children sweeping,
Children whispering

(End of lunch)
Children burping!

Ellis Rogers (9)
Wood End Park Community School

Sun And Clouds

The sun is hot and burning
nice hot area, beautiful colour,
yellow beaming in the sky,
round ball glowing high.
Clouds are beautiful,
white, puffy like cotton wool.
Dark, heaving with rain,
this causes the weather
to be a pain.

Iveta Olahova (11)
Wood End Park Community School

The Dog And The Pussycat

(Based on 'The Owl And The Pussycat' by Edward Lear)

The dog and the pussycat went to the park,
On an old, black, rusty scooter.
They each bought a spud with a can of mud,
In a bag with a mini computer.
The pussy looked at the climbing frame
And sang herself a tune,
'Oh up above so round you are,
I wish I could walk on you moon,
Oh moon,
Oh moon,
One day I will walk on you moon!'

Dog frowned at Pussy, 'Who are you singing to,
You never sing to me!
Oh how rude you are, I'm buying a car,
And I'll go and live by the sea!'
So he drove away for an hour a day
To the soft, golden sand
And there in the sky,
His pussy flew by,
Flew by,
Flew by,
There the poor pussy flew by.

'Dear Pussy I didn't know you could fly,'
'Oh I can't!' cried the pussy, 'I can't!
I was on the swing, when I saw a gold ring,
Then it chucked me into the plant!'
So the dog and the pussy went back home
And had their spud with the mud,
But the dog took one bite and to his delight,
It tasted like English fudge,
The sludge,
The sludge,
It tasted like English fudge.

Kayleigh Bowdrey (11)
Wood End Park Community School

A Shining Star

As I gaze into the sky;
The stars wink at me, as though to smile.
Waving and laughing;
Dancing with glee.
The stars twinkle
And sing a silent song.
Some in groups as though gossiping
And as I get into bed,
They bid me farewell.

Daniel Miles
Wood End Park Community School

Day And Night

Day
Sunny, bright
Waking, playing, shopping
Sleeping, dreaming, snoring
Stars, dark
Night.

David Watford (10)
Wood End Park Community School

Sea

The lovely, hot sun in the red sky
as it goes down all the seagulls come out to play
and the turtles come out to shore.
The yellow beach and the children running around
and enjoying themselves with their mums and dads.

Reece Saunders (10)
Wood End Park Community School

On The Playground

Children running,
Children jumping,
Children skipping,
Skipping, skipping.

Children playing,
Children laughing,
Children talking, talking, talking.

Children smiling,
Children hopping,
Children screaming,
Screaming, screaming.

Bell goes, children stopping.

Nadine Bowen (8)
Wood End Park Community School

On The Playground

Children bumping,
Children thumping
Children jumping, jumping, jumping

Children sweeping,
Children peeping,
Children creeping, creeping, creeping.

Children hopping,
Children stopping,
Children stropping, stropping, stropping.

End of the playground
Children leaving.

Teleasha Bogle (8)
Wood End Park Community School

At The Swimming Pool

Children swimming,
Adults wringing,
People diving, diving, diving,

Children jumping,
Adults thumping,
People bumping, bumping, bumping.

Children racing,
Adults chasing,
People dashing, dashing, dashing.

Lifeguard blows the whistle,
Everyone gets out.

Luke Innes (9)
Wood End Park Community School

On The Playground

Children bumping,
Children thumping,
Children jumping, jumping, jumping.

Children weeping,
Children creeping,
Children leaping, leaping, leaping.

Children talking,
Children walking,
Children stalking, stalking, stalking.

Ding-a-ling-a-ling
(Bell goes) children stop.

Macayla Benoit (9)
Wood End Park Community School

Witch Itch

There was a witch
Who had a terrible itch.

Her name was Bubble,
She was in itchy trouble.

Bubble used potions
And of course lotions.

She tried all sorts of things,
Even the forbidden one with diamond rings.

It got worse,
She was in need of a nurse.

Her friend opened the door,
She fell flat on the floor.

They told her to rest in bed
And then Bubble said,

'Atchoo, atchoo, atchoo!'
And the witch doctor said,
'You've got the itchy flu!'

Amber Cooley (11)
Wood End Park Community School

Never Play Hide-And-Seek
With A Giraffe

Never play hide-and-seek with a giraffe,
All they do is cheat,
When you go to hide,
They leap out with their long necks
And start to peek.

When you think you've found a good place,
Well you would be wrong,
They would already know where you are!

Charlene Svinurayi
Wood End Park Community School

On The Football Pitch

Strikers kicking,
Strikers heading
Strikers dribbling, dribbling, dribbling.

Strikers scoring,
Strikers passing,
Strikers panting, panting, panting.

Strikers huffing,
Strikers puffing,
Strikers shaking, shaking, shaking.

The full-time whistle goes,
Strikers huffing and puffing.

Suraj Davdra (9)
Wood End Park Community School

Frosty The Snowman

Frosty the snowman comes this year
And makes the ice very clear,
Then comes his evil twin,
Who won't go away until he wins,
He makes a blizzard and cracks the ice,
Then all the people aren't very nice.
He goes and thinks he's won this year
But he's wrong,
Everyone's happy except for him
And he has to wait until next year!

Lakiesha Griffith
Wood End Park Community School

Teachers

Our teacher always bites off our heads
And whenever she shouts her face goes quite red.
She always makes us boys get in trouble,
Maybe one day she will pop like a bubble.

Sometimes I feel like dialling 999,
She makes us sit there and cry and whine.
Sometimes I feel like I want to die,
Say to my parents, 'Goodbye,'

Her face is ringing around my head,
I always think about that when I go to bed.
She always tries to act all bad,
But all she does is make us sad.

She tries to act like Mr Blair,
But she can't get anything really clear.
She talks like she is Mr Bush,
She gives our luck a big push.

Vijay Kocher (11)
Wood End Park Community School

The Sky

Up in the sky the birds are flying,
When you look down the baby is crying.
The sky is blue and the baby hasn't got a clue.
Up in the sky the birds are flying,
When you look down the baby is crying!

Saira Mushtaq (10)
Wood End Park Community School

Stars

Bright, shimmering in the sky,
A diamond flickering up and high,
When it falls it walks and shines,
Up in the sky with silver lines,
Shining upon the river lies,
When it sees you it flickers by.

Watching upon your house it shines,
Walking by, keeping an eye,
Keeping light till day and night,
Making sure it shines its light,
When it's sunrise it's time to go,
Just to make sure it keeps its glow.

Payal Patel (10)
Wood End Park Community School

I Want To Be A Poet

I want to be a poet,
Most people do not know it.
I try and I try
But the ideas
Just pass me by.
Maybe someday
I will be able to say
I wrote that, I did
Although I'm just a kid.

Samantha Jayne Salmon (10)
Wood End Park Community School

The Haunted Treasure

As the moon rises and its light fills the sky,
The eerie sight of the skull and crossbones goes by.
The evil pirates cross the salty sea,
Searching for where the precious treasure may be.

It's the Forbidden Island that they seek,
Hidden beyond the haunted creek.
The captain orders the men to keep on rowing,
Off in the distance he's seen something glowing.

As the ship draws near to land,
They can practically feel the gold in their hand.

The ship drops anchor; the pirates cheer,
Not realising there is yet much to fear.
For there is a curse on those who try,
To steal the gold; their fate . . . *to die.*

Shane Gill Mann (11)
Wood End Park Community School

Snow

Crickle, crackle treads the ice,
It is slippery and it is not nice.
As the chilly, frozen icicles drop onto the floor,
Children leave the door and play some more.

Snow falling, snowman building
Flakes are falling crystal clear,
While men warm and cosy are
Watching football, drinking beer.

Daisy Dark (11)
Wood End Park Community School

The Sea

The sea is crystal,
Clear as glass.
It is relaxing,
When I stroll past.

The sea is salty,
With its misty face.
When the white horses pass,
At a slow, soft pace.

The sea glimmers,
In the sun's light.
There goes the storm
And a crash with light.

The sea crashes,
Hard against the rocks.
The boats all shake,
In their docks.

Chloe George (11)
Wood End Park Community School

I Wanna

I wanna be a superstar,
Like my mother.
I wanna drive a big car,
Like my father.
I wanna be a motorbike racer,
Like my brother.
I wanna be a super, beautiful
Kid.

Kayleigh Blackmore (10)
Wood End Park Community School

The Sea

The sea is a fantastic thing
It crashes against the stones
Clear as a blue crystal
I love the sea
A breath of fresh air
Seagulls flying in the bright blue
The sea full of wonderful creatures
I love the sea.

Kathleen Cassidy (11)
Wood End Park Community School

Chair In The Corner

There he sits in the corner
All alone on four little legs
Nobody will sit on him
Because he's all worn out
Then a kid comes along
To sit on him
Now he's used and happy again.

Joseph McGeough (11)
Wood End Park Community School

Sea Poem

As I walked along the sand,
Rolling waves crashed against the rocks.

The sun set, it went calm, it was clear, cool.
The moonlight shone on the calm, freezing water.

Hannah White (10)
Wood End Park Community School

Sea Poem

A cool, clear, crystal sea
No white horses yet
Freezing, ripple, moody, grey
Stormy sky, sea rises up stronger.

White horses, vicious waves,
Storm begins.

An ebbing tide
In and out will chase
The seagulls right out.

Rachael Tuckwell (11)
Wood End Park Community School

Sea

Salty, clear
Moving, splashing, evaporating
Blowing, racing, surviving
Hot, deserted
Desert.

Priya Kumar (10)
Wood End Park Community School

The Sea

Children splashing, water here and there,
Waves twisting and turning,
Crabs crawling to and fro,
And the sun, hot and burning.

Dolphins gliding peacefully,
The sand, golden and bright,
And starfish in rocky pools,
It's such a lovely sight.

Neha Kochhar (11)
Wood End Park Community School

The Mystic World

The mystic world is a giant balloon,
Overcrowded with idiotic buffoons,
Waterfalls are giant taps,
The mountains wear thick snowcaps,
And the fluffy clouds are cotton buds,
The rocks are overgrown spuds,
The trees' branches stretch out like towers,
These are all the mystic world's powers.

Rukhsar Ahmed (10)
Wood End Park Community School

The Sea

The sea is so calm, crystal clear
Water overlapping against the rocks
People splashing and enjoying themselves
Tides coming in and out
The sand is so tender
Young children making sandcastles
Different shapes of shells lying on the smooth sand.

Seema Dhiman (11)
Wood End Park Community School

The Sea

Sea creatures floating, swimming,
In the deep blue sea,
Dolphins in the deep blue sea,
Jumping and diving,
Starfish on the beach,
Glittering in the sunshine.

Joseph Hikwa (11)
Wood End Park Community School

The World

The sea is blue
The grass is green
The roses are red
A river grows from a stream
Daffodils are yellow
The sunset is orange, red and mellow
The bluebells are a violet
The world keeps growing.

Sian Olds (10)
Wood End Park Community School

Snow Falling

Snow falling gently down to the ground,
Snowflakes spinning and twisting in the wintry sky,
Setting and crystallising on the wintry floor,
Children slipping and sliding across the icy carpet.

Jack Dent
Wood End Park Community School

Summer And Winter

Hot, sunny
Boiling, sunbathing, drinking
Snowing, shivering, freezing,
Blizzard, windy,
Winter.

Tommy Mulligan (11)
Wood End Park Community School

The Mission In The Restaurant

They went to a restaurant,
and chose the table in front.
Their mission had failed,
for they got blackmailed.
So they ran for their lives,
for they had Nike fives,
Nike fives,
Nike fives.
But they needed Nike tens,
for they were as slow as hens,
as hens,
as hens.
So they got caught,
being five dollars short!

Babar Shariff (11)
Wood End Park Community School

Hide-And-Seek

Vicky is small,
she will find a tiny place.
Samantha is noisy,
you'll hear her a mile away.
Walk slowly,
you'll be able to hear someone
moving or breathing heavily.
You hear someone moving,
Vicky.
You smell something sickly,
Vicky again.
You go and look somewhere else,
then you see Samantha peeping out
from her hiding place,
which is always behind the curtain.

Hayley Smith (11)
Wood End Park Community School

Sea And Desert

Salty, clear
Moving, splashing, evaporating
Blowing, racing, swimming
Hot, deserted.

Sara Piper (10)
Wood End Park Community School

A Shark

The shark has teeth like steel,
If he bites you he won't even feel,
He'll rip your head off,
And make your blood cough,
So he does not fear,
Because he doesn't even care.

Thomas Sharma
Wood End Park Community School

Day

Sunny, bright
Waking, playing, shopping
Sleeping, dreaming, snoring
Stars, dark
Night.

Jake Smith (10)
Wood End Park Community School